What readers say

"I did decide to self publish and my novel, Kindergarten Karma, took first place in the Writer's Digest National Self-published Book Award, best mainstream/literary fiction category." (Dionna Day, San Francisco, CA)

"..really enjoyed your class on marketing books and have adapted your ideas to my difficult to market "niche book" with great success." (Patricia Bobeck, Geologist, Austin, TX)

"...most expert I have ever met...packed so much hands-on information..." Ronald Bacchiocchi, Portsmouth, RI)

"...I was motivated and challenged. The "plan" for writing one's book is superb...loads of info packed into each moment." (Lynn Cooper, Chicago, IL)

"...down to earth, realistic, with lots of suggestions, advice, company names, etc." (Danette Wagner, Twin Falls, ID)

"...concise, clear, and very informative." (Sharon & John Curry, Independence, MO)

"I have been to some other workshops and while they were good, they didn't come close to providing the kind of detail and information that you provided...I now have an understanding of the process and strategy." (Debra Fehr Heindel, Sacramento, CA)

"...just what I needed. I have finished my first book and received my first acceptance for one of my camping articles...I am so happy! I learned a wealth of information..." (Karen Gavis, Dallas, TX)

Writing, Publishing & Marketing Your 1st Book (or 7th)
© 2007

Bobbie Christensen

EFFECTIVE LIVING PUBLISHING
P. O. Box 232233
Sacramento, CA 95823
ELPBooks@aol.com

Published by Effective Living Publishing
P.O.Box 232233, Sacramento, CA 95823
(916) 422-8435; orders (800) 929-7889
Email: ELPBooks@aol.com
Website: www.BooksAmerica.com

Cover design by Mustang Graphic Designers
www.MustangGFX.com
MustangGraphic@aol.com
(916) 422-7109

ISBN: 978-0-9729173-4-6

TABLE OF CONTENTS

Books by Bobbie and Eric Christensen
Building Your Financial Portfolio On $25 A Month (Or Less), 4th Edition ($15.95)
Adding To Your Financial Portfolio, 2nd Edition ($15.95)
Top 50 Best Stock Investments, 2nd Edition ($19.95)
Building Your Debt-Free Life ($14.95)
Smart Real Estate Investing ($15.95)
Retiring Healthy, Wealthy & Wise ($12.95)

Common Sense Portfolio newsletter ($26 for 1 year, $47 for 2 years)

Books by Bobbie Christensen
Building Your Dream Life: Career, Sex & Leisure, 2nd Edition ($14.95)
The Banker Chronicles, a mystery ($14.95)
Writing, Publishing & Marketing Your 1st Book (or 7th) On A Shoe-String Budget ($15.95)

Books by Eric Christensen
Fly Fishing For Fun ($15.95)

Add $4 for shipping and handling per order.
To order, call 1-800-929-7889 (Mastercard & Visa accepted)
Or mail check or money order to:
BooksAmerica, PO Box 232233, Sacramento, CA 95823
Or order online at www.BooksAmerica.com
Prices guaranteed through 12/07

Introduction

Welcome to the new updated first published edition of Writing, Publishing & Marketing Your 1st Book (or 7th) On A Shoe-String Budget. Some of you are already familiar with this publication in booklet form which just goes to show you that you can successfully publish booklets as well as books! However, in order to make this information available to many people who, not being able to attend a class, tried to purchase this at a bookstore or get it at their library, we are now publishing it in book form.

All of the information in this book has been created and gathered to accompany the nationwide seminars presented by Bobbie Christensen for potential writers and published authors. Thousands of writers have already used its step-by-step approach to successfully write, publish and market their own books. All writers are creative people and their works show this individuality, but in the writing section of this book you will learn how to (and why to) create a page-turner whether you are writing a fiction or non-fiction, a mystery or a textbook. Also, this book contains all the information, forms, and examples you will need to either submit your work to a publisher or to self-publish and then teaches you an easy and inexpensive 6-step marketing plan that has been proven successful with hundreds of writers. At the request of many seminar attendees, we have also included a fourth section on traveling on a shoe-string budget because the more you can travel the more books you will sell.

Bobbie has been a freelance writer for over 30 years and has successfully self-published ten books to date including best-sellers and award-winners. Her purpose in writing this book (and presenting the seminars) is to share what took her several years to learn (the hard way) so that your success may

1

come more quickly and easily. However, the most important reason for this book is to give you all the information you need in order to make a logical decision about your book - - should you write it or not. Writing a book is the easy part but there is a lot of hard work involved in publishing and particularly in marketing your book and the only way you can make a good decision for yourself and your book is by having all the necessary information. If you are unable to attend a seminar with Bobbie, the complete six hours is also available on audio CD's (through BooksAmerica.com or call 1-800-929-7889).

Please be aware that anyone who attends a seminar or purchases this book is allowed free consulting with the author at any time. If you have a question or need help with anything, just email Bobbie at ELPBooks@aol.com.

Good luck!

Bobbie Christensen

Sacramento, CA
January 2007

PART I – Writing Your 1st Book (or 7th)

There are a lot of methods for writing a book. I created the following method for myself many years ago but refused to teach it because I thought it was a weird way of writing. However, after several years of students in Publishing & Marketing Your Book asking for help in the actual writing, and after finding that these people were actually able to quickly finish their books using my method, I started offering it to everyone.

You will be using my own step-by-step method to "build" a book one layer at a time. There are a few things you will need in order to start your writing business and things you will need to know. In order to be successful at any business, you must become organized. You will need a calendar, preferably one where each month is on one page and each day is about one inch by one inch giving you just enough room to know what you are supposed to do on this day. As of May 1st of each year, you will need a calendar for the next year for marketing purposes. You will also need a stack of index cards.

Some of you have been dreaming for years of writing a book and some of you have been working for yeas on a particular book. Well, it is now time to actually do it! Using the following method, you will complete your manuscript ready for printing in 6 weeks. If you work full time and can only work on weekends, you will complete your manuscript in about 20 weekends. Therefore, you need to (1) mark on the calendar the date you are actually going to start your book and then (2) count up six weeks (or 20 weekends) and put "manuscript complete". Keep in mind that you must know the exact day your manuscript will be complete. You will find out why in Part II on Publishing Your Book. Keeping a calendar is extremely important in any business. Writing a book is a business and you are the boss.

You also need to figure out what time you will go to work. You need to figure out whether you are a morning person, an afternoon person, or a night person and then mark you calendar which days of the week you will be working and at what time. Remember that this is your business and you are the boss. That means you have to set your own time schedule because no one else is going to do it for you. If you do not set a time schedule for yourself, you will either never finish your book or it will take you ten years to do so.

Before starting the 10 steps for writing your book, please read the following hints for helping you to write.

1. As a writer, you need to find a quiet place to work where no one will disturb you. Writing is creative work and you will need peace and quiet. No one should disturb you short of the house being on fire. And, if someone does yell "The house is on fire", remember to take your work with you! As silly as it sounds, please back up your work every day. I do not know of a single writer, including myself, who has not at one time or another lost an entire manuscript. Back up your work!

2. You are now a writer! When someone asks you, "What do you do?" you answer, "I'm a writer!" Your mind set has a lot to do with your success no matter what your business is. However, thinking of yourself as a writer starting today will also affect the sales of your new book.

3. Write everything down! As a creative and imaginative person, you get lots of ideas for characters and story lines. The average person forgets even very important

4

ideas within five minutes so write your ideas down immediately. Keep paper and pen wherever an idea might come to you (in the bedroom, kitchen, by the TV, in the car, and office) and keep these thoughts in an "idea file". This Idea File can come in handy even with your first book.

4. Do your research. Never try to fool your reader because you will always find someone who knows the subject very well and will be happy to send you a nasty note pointing out your mistake. This is not to say that we are perfect. We all make mistakes. Let's just try to keep them to a minimum. Also, I do not count research time as part of writing because research time varies from one person to another and from one book to another. You could be writing about something you have done for years and can sit down right now and start writing. However, you could be writing something that you need to do a little or a lot of research on. Therefore, set an amount of time you will allow for research and put that on your calendar before the day you have marked for starting your manuscript.

5. Do not try to copy anyone else's style of writing. Always write in your own voice. This is creating your own style. But don't be afraid to read other people's work and learn from them. You will learn a lot of things from the writers you like but you will learn even more by reading the authors you don't like.

6. Do not worry about how many pages your manuscript is. If it ends up being more than 60 pages, you can get it published as a book. If it ends up less, you can still publish it as a booklet. If you decide to sell your work to a publisher, keep in mind that they all have their own set of rules (how many chapters per book, how many pages per chapter, etc.). As you cannot possibly write a book to meet

the requirements of all the different publishers, for now write your book to please yourself. If a publisher does buy it, you will then be required to rewrite it to meet their specifications anyway.

Now let's get started on that book you have always dreamed of.

1. Creating Your Story

Some writers start with characters rather than a story line but, for the beginner or anyone who finds themselves taking far too long to complete their manuscript, it is easier to start with the story. A story usually starts as a one or two sentence description of an idea you have. That's simple enough. Write these 2 or 3 sentences on the first index card and tape it on the wall above where you work to remind you of where you are going with this book. These few sentences need to tell what the main question of the story is going to be (will she find her love, will the earth be saved, will the reader know how to have a happier life after reading this book). Some writers will have a second question (second story line) also (will she find her love and solve the mystery of who killed her brother, will the earth be saved and the hero and heroine get together at the end, what did the writer have to go through to discover how to have a happier life). You will grow this two sentence description into a storyline.

This one card should take you only about 15 minutes. However, do not start the next step yet. You want to spend one night tossing and turning and thinking about your story so that the next day you can add or subtract from the story you created yesterday.

2. Creating Scenes

No matter what type of book you are writing, you will be covering several areas. That is, a non-fiction book about fire safety will be covering a lot of different areas such as home safety, keeping kids safe, kitchen safety, etc. Or a work of fiction will cover how did they meet, what is the mystery they have to solve, how is it resolved, etc. Each of these areas will be a separate scene. Some books (particulary non-fiction) will have each scene be a whole chapter while other books (fiction) will have several scenes within a chapter. Do not worry about chapters right now. You just want to think about each scene.

A scene is whenever you change location or time in your story and each scene must have a question. That is, the maid finding the dead body and screaming is one scene and then you switch scenes to the police investigating the crime. If writing a fiction, the question may or may not have an answer in this scene. If writing non-fiction, usually you will answer the question by the end of the scene. For instance, if writing about quitting smoking and explaining a particular method in this scene, you will also have the answer (how it works, etc.) within the scene.

I firmly believe every book, whether fiction, non-fiction, children's, cookbook, or textbook must be a page turner. You do not want to bore your readers to death. You want them to enjoy the reading experience and tell their friends about your book. In order to make any book interesting and a real page turner, each scene must include something interesting. However, the problem comes at the end of each chapter (which we will talk about later). How do you keep your reader from finishing a chapter and then going to bed? You want to keep your readers sleepless!

So to create scenes, you will take one index card and write on it how this book begins, what is the first scene. Keep in mind that the first scene and, in fact, the first paragraph should contain "what is the most important thing I am trying to do with this book". Then take the next index card and write where the book goes from there. Then the third card takes the book along through another scene. You need to outline your entire book from beginning to end, one scene at a time. The reason so many people spend so long writing a book is because they do not take the time to outline the entire book to know where they are going. Thus, you spend all of your time staring off into space trying to think of what to write next. A good outline will save you a lot of time.

When you think about writing a book, you usually spend a lot of time thinking about one part or a couple of parts of your book (the guts of the book) but do not bother with other scenes such as how to start the book or how to get to the big culmination of the story. Therefore, some scene cards will have a lot of information on them and some will have very little.

Each scene must include certain information. First, what is the question being asked in this scene. Whether you are writing fiction or non-fiction, each scene must have a question that needs to be answered. For example, (cookbook) why are pasta sauces in northern Italy different from those in southern Italy and then use the recipes to explain the differences. Or (traveling) deciding what you want to see and do on vacation, deciding what your budget will allow, how to stretch your budget further, etc. Or (fiction) a man believes his brother was murdered even though the police say it was simply a car accident, the man meets with a woman doctor for autopsy information but finds out the wife refused to allow an autopsy, the man along with the woman doctor (romantic interest) go to the wife for information but find a young man there with her, etc.

That is, each scene (which may or may not be a whole chapter) must be asking a question. Each question must find an answer (even in non-fiction). In a mystery, each question may be answered but only creates another question (the next scene) to find the answer to. In a non-fiction, readers want answers to their questions (how to create wealth, how to solve the problem of criminal Congresspeople, etc.) That is, do not write a book that just complains about something. People want answers! They already know what the problem is!

In each scene keep in mind the old phrase journalists use: who, what, when, where, why and how. In fiction, the main characters need to be introduced right away in either the first or second scene. In non-fiction, where you might be using different characters throughout your book, the characters will be introduced as needed throughout the book.

You will write a basic idea for each scene on a separate index card, from the beginning of your book all the way to the end, and tape these scenes on the wall where you can see them. Keep in mind that the reason for using index cards is that they can be easily changed. That is, if you are writing and don't like this scene here, you can always move it to another location, or you can easily take out scenes or add more scenes as needed.

There is one more card you need to complete. Today most books have introductions because it can solve quite a few writing problems. So you will take one index card and write at the top "introduction" and outline what needs to be in your introduction.

First of all, if you are writing a biography or autobiography (something that happened in your life or your families life or your business life), I highly recommend doing it as a work of fiction if at all possible. You could be writing about the horrible boss you once worked for but you don't want him to sue you for defamation of character. Therefore, you need to fictionalize the story. He may know that you wrote the book and recognizes himself in your book, but in a court of law he must be able to prove that others can recognize him in your book and that the book hurts him in some way (he loses business, loses his wife, etc.)

More importantly, however, is that your book can only be in one category in a bookstore or library and very few people go into a store and immediately head for the biography section. Most readers head for the fiction section. Therefore, if you can write your book as fiction, you will have the chance for a lot more potential buyers to at least see your book. This does not mean that you can't let people know your book is based on real life. For instance, in my book, *The Banker Chronicles*. I have an introduction that says basically, "Everything in this book is based on things that actually happened to me, my husband, or our friends while working in banking but it is done as a work of fiction to protect the innocent."

If you have changed characters names or any other information in a non-fiction (factual) book, you need to let your reader know in this introduction. For instance, you are writing about your clients but some of them do not want you using their real names so you will say, "Some identities have been changed to protect the individuals.".

Also a lot of non-fiction writers have a tendency to begin their books with "why I'm writing this book". This is boring to the reader who just wants to start learning this instant. Therefore, put the "why" in your introduction. Start the actual book by jumping right into the story.

It should take you about 2 days to outline all of the scenes from beginning to end and keep in mind that these are not carved in granite. You can change your mind any time you want to by taking out scenes or adding scenes.

People write books for one of two reasons. Either you have a great story to tell and want to entertain readers with it (fiction) or you have something you want to teach people (non-fiction). If you are really good, you combine the two by entertaining and teaching at the same time. However, no matter how good your story is, you need characters your reader can empathize with or care about.

3. Creating Living Characters

In order to learn what you are trying to teach or to care about your story, the audience must have characters they care about. This applies to fiction and non-fiction. Most fiction writers realize you have to have characters with a problem to solve but a lot of non-fiction writers tend to forget about characters. In order for a reader to learn what you are trying to teach them, they need to have at least one character they can associate with. Even if you are writing about your own history, you need to have other characters in your story so that it is not just a self-centered book.

For instance, if you are writing a cook book, it will be an enjoyable read and draw your reader in if you talk about where each recipe came from using examples of other people

11

(your grandmother cooking on an old wood stove). However, you can take this even further by telling your grandmother's history, where she grew up, how she met Grampa, etc. In other words, create your characters so the reader will know them and care about them.

You will have an index card for each character. First, you need to name the character. If the name is very unusual, I suggest you have the name sounded out in parenthesis the first time you use it. It is annoying to the reader to keep stumbling over how this name is pronounced. If she is based on a real person, put the fictional name first and then the real person's name in parenthesis so you don't forget who you are talking about. If using real people in a non-fiction, remember that you must have written permission to use them in your book. If they refuse, you will need to change their names and descriptions and backgrounds so they cannot be easily recognized by the reading public.

Second, you need to write a physical description of each character. Make sure each one looks different so the reader can easily imagine this character. Writing this down will be easier then making a mistake such as changing the characters eyes that began as brown to blue by the end of the book.

Third, you need to write a biography of the character. Your reader cannot care about this character unless you make him an individual. Think of it in terms of a weekly TV show. If all the actors in the sitcom have bland personalities and you know nothing about their background, the show flops. A series like "Two and a Half Men" has a cast wherein each character has a different personality and different background.

Fourth, you need a reason why this character is in the story. What is their purpose.

The easiest way to find interesting characters is to look around you. Look at the members of your family, your friends and co-workers, people you see in a restaurant. Pick out the little idiosyncrasies that make them interesting and different.

Keep in mind that using your characters correctly can easily lead the reader to your next book. For instance, if Missy is the lead character solving a murder, does she have a friend, Christy, who is helping her yet always finding fault with her boss at work? Perhaps Missy suggests her friend start her own business to get away from that boss. This can carry Christy into the lead of her own book. The same thing applies to non-fiction. If you are writing a cook book and describe one particular pasta dish, you might also say, "Of course, Italy is famous for pasta, but describing all of those would take another whole book!" This gives you the opportunity to write a second book.

Remember that you are writing to entertain your audience. People write books either to entertain or to teach. However, if you are really good, you combine teaching and entertaining. Not only will the reader enjoy a story that is entertaining but a non-fiction reader will enjoy and remember your important lesson if they are being entertained.

Again, if you are writing something biographical or autobiographical, I highly suggest you write it as a work of fiction in order to prevent law suits and to get your book into the fictional section of the book store or library where more readers will be able to see it.

Each character will be on a separate index card and taped above your scene cards. You should be able to complete your character cards in two days keeping in mind that you can add or subtract characters as you are writing.

It should take you about 2 days to complete your character list. Now you have your entire book outlined and your characters ready to go. Now you need to build your story.

4. Writing Your Book

The biggest problem writers have is actually getting started on a new book. Just saying, "Some day I'm going to write a book," will never get it done. The second biggest problem is sitting at that computer the first day and thinking, "Where should I start, what should I say," and wasting a lot of time. However, you have already solved that problem by creating a good outline. And you will complete this step in just 10 days so mark it on your calendar!

When you sit down to write, instead of being overwhelmed by trying to write a whole book, take the first scene off the wall, put it right in front of you, and just write that one scene. Do not think about where this is all going, just write this one scene. It is like writing a little short story with this scene having its own question.

Obviously the very first scene is where you need to grab the reader. You need to decide the most important thing you want your reader to get from your book and introduce that right in the first scene. In other words, you are letting the reader know what this book is about. For instance, the murder mystery may have the girl finding the dead body (something dramatic to catch the reader's attention). If writing that non-fiction about quitting smoking, you would be talking about the first method you want to teach them in that first scene but, in order to catch the reader's attention, you might start by describing Joe holding his sobbing wife as he tells her he has cancer. If writing about your life (or someone else's), you need to decide what is the most important thing you want people to get from this book and put that in the very first scene.

What creates a good page turner is having each scene give the reader a good story with a question that will be answered (either in this scene or by the end of the book). What creates a good chapter is ending it with a question that leads into the next chapter. For example, in a fiction Missy questions the police and finds that her brother died from an apparent heart attack but she knows he just had a complete physical and had no heart problem. Thus the question becomes could something have caused the heart attack, who else can she talk to for more information, what information does she need? If writing that non-fiction cook book, you will be teaching the recipe but also telling the story behind the recipe such as where did you get this recipe, did a little old woman in Italy give you her family recipe, can this recipe be done in a healthier way? However, you still need to end the chapter with a question to lead the reader into the next chapter. Perhaps something like, "My grandmother firmly believed in hearty meals for her farmer husband. However, he died at 50 from a heart attack. Can we still enjoy these hearty meals but in a more healthy manner?" And this leads into healthy main courses.

Let's say you have finished that first scene and are feeling quite good about it. So you put the scene back on the wall and take down the second scene. Now you want to just write this scene. Do not worry about where this book is going, just write this scene as though you are writing another short story. You will keep doing one scene at a time all the way to the end of your book. However, you can't write an entire book in one day. At some point you will find yourself brain-dead, you just cannot write another creative word today. Let's say you managed to write 10 pages that first day. At this point you need to back up your work, write yourself a short note of where you left off, and leave for the day. Get a good night's rest.

When you start writing your book, you will find out something very interesting about yourself. That is, how long can you write each day before you are brain dead! This happens to everyone. You get to that point where you just can't think of what you are trying to write. At this point, you will find out how long you can work on your book each day and the length of time will vary for each of you. Some people can write for 5 or 6 hours before they have to quit for the day and some can only write for 1 or 2 hours. However long you lasted on the first day of writing will be how long you can last each day thereafter. Knowing this will make it easier for you to schedule your writing day. Keep in mind that the times for each section I am giving you are based on my own writing of 10 pages a day. If you are slower, just increase the writing time from 10 days to 20 days - - but no longer! We want to get this book done!

The biggest problem writers have is going in to work on your book the next day and re-reading what you wrote the previous day to see where you left off. If you do this, you will automatically start rewriting and by the end of the second day you are still on page 10! Maybe by day three you manage to get to page 11! The problem is that, unless you have a photographic memory, you cannot remember where you left off. So, even though it is inherent in all of us, you must force

16

yourself to not look at the previous pages. You must force yourself to start on page 11 without looking at even the last paragraph you wrote. Otherwise you will take ten years to write this book!

What you will do is take the note you wrote to yourself of where you left off and go from there. Do not look at the last paragraph or even the last sentence! Yes, there will be problems, things you left out, but you will correct these problems later. The most important thing now is to get the entire story down on paper and to do it quickly. You will correct the mistakes and problems later. One reason for doing this is to keep your creativity fresh. If you re-read those first 10 pages, you are now tied down to what you were writing yesterday. But what if you had a great new idea during the night? Also, remember that your mood each day will affect your writing. You may end up with each section being in a different mood but you can decide later exactly what mood you want this book to be in. For now, just get this book done!

A quick note on ending a book - - sad endings are critically acclaimed, but happy endings sell a lot more books!

As you concentrate on each scene, write quickly not worrying about details. Just let the words flow. We need to get this book done. For one thing, if you want to become a full time writer some day, you cannot have five years between books because your readers and the media will completely forget about you. You need to be able to get a new book out at least every two years.

When you have written the last scene, you will now build your book one layer at a time. The first layer will be dialogue. You might be very good at dialogue and were including a lot of dialogue as you wrote your book, but do _not_

17

skip this step. No matter what you have included while originally writing your book, do not skip any of the following steps. In fact, if you are reading this and have already finished your entire manuscript, I would suggest you start with the next step.

5. Creating Dialogue

All books need at least some dialogue. Some books will have a lot of dialogue. However, a man's action adventure might have only a little dialogue.

Now that you have your entire manuscript, you are going to build it into a good book one layer at a time starting with dialogue. Keep in mind that *dialogue must move the story along.* Take the sentence, "I hate walking in the rain." Does this mean something in the story? Does it help identify the character speaking as a person who is lazy or does not like the outdoors? Or does this sentence lead up to finding a gold coin that the rain has washed the dirt from so it could be found? In other words, dialogue must accomplish something. If it does not, then leave it out.

Do not create unnecessary dialogue. As in any good movie, you need to keep your storyline tight to keep the readers attention.

Remember that dialogue is both the spoken word (as in quoted dialogue) and the thought process. That is, sometimes it is better to use your own thought process to describe what is happening rather than having two people talking through the whole episode.

Do not use a lot of "he said" phrases. If you have created each character with a different personality, you should be able to do a two-way conversation (between two of the characters) without having to state who is speaking because their personalities and the role they play in the story will show in what they are saying.

Now you are ready to create the dialogue in your book (even if you have already put in a lot of dialogue). Start on page one of your manuscript and read through the entire book concentrating only on creating good dialogue that moves the story along. You wrote your entire manuscript and now you will be adding one layer at a time beginning with dialogue.

However, as you are working on the dialogue you will also be re-writing. This is your first re-write. You will be finding those problem areas where you picked up writing the next day and forgot what you had been saying the day before. You will see where you changed the story for a better story line and will need to change some things to tie in with this one. You will see the different moods you wrote in each day and will need to decide which mood you want your book to be in. But always remember that you are concentrating on dialogue. As you finish re-writing a section, you must go back to working on the dialogue. If you have to, put a note in front of you saying "dialogue" so you will remember what you are working on.

NOTE: Think of the most popular movies ever done. Do they have dialogue in them?

It should take you about two to four days (depending on how fast a writer you are) to go through your entire book working on dialogue and doing your first re-write. Now we have to make sure the reader does not get bored and fall asleep.

19

6. Creating Action, Adventure, Interest

Some books will have a lot of action and adventure and some books will have just a little, but all books need some in order to keep your reader interested. This is just as important for non-fiction as fiction so the reader doesn't stop at the end of a chapter and never finish reading your book.

Part of the action/adventure is created through your story as you need to have an interesting story to begin with. Some of the action adventure can be created through your dialogue as in creating tension between two people or providing more information about the mystery or providing clues or making the reader wonder if this character is telling the truth or not. But another way is to write scenes with action and adventure. There is the obvious action scene wherein the hero comes to blows with an unknown (at this point) attacker, or the brakes on the heroine's car fail, or she wakes in the middle of the night to the sound of breaking glass. However, non-fiction also needs action adventure in order to keep the reader's attention.

If you are writing about fire safety, you need a good example of what people are feeling when going through a fire. If you are writing a cook book, tell the reader how you almost burned down your house one day. Every book needs some action/adventure to keep your reader interested.

This is also the prime way to make readers turn the page. That is, rather than finish the chapter with, "...and that is how you make homemade bread," finish that chapter with something that will drag the reader into the next chapter. For instance, you are talking about the funny customers you have experienced and want the next chapter to be about more serious customer situations. Perhaps you could lead into it (in the last paragraph of the previous chapter) with something like, "Then there was Sharon. She called because her luggage had been lost containing her wedding dress and the wedding was the next day!" You need something so the reader wants to continue reading to find out what happened. Did she get her wedding dress in time?

You will add this action/adventure layer by reading your book again, starting on page one, and concentrating this time only on adding action, adventure and interest. And, yes, this will be your second rewrite.

NOTE: Do the most popular movies have action adventure in them?

You should allow about two to four days for this step.

Everyone needs some action and adventure to keep their interest but remember that 90% of all books are bought by women and women like a little romance in their lives.

7. Creating Romance

A lot of writers automatically think their cook book or text book has no romance in it. However, what we mean is anything from a very strong relationship between two people to an actual romance. Have you gone through your entire life without a single close relationship of some kind? After all, you are writing a book about life and having close relationships are a part of life. You can use close relationships to define your characters better, to create more interest in what you are trying to teach, to make your reader care about your book.

Romance covers a broad spectrum from caring about your best friend and how do you show that in action and/or words all the way to the actual sex act. You need to decide how much relationship you want in your book keeping in mind that every book needs some.

Romance and relationships can be used to create more tension and interest in the storyline. Does the relationship between three friends in the Harry Potter books create more tension and interest? Keep in mind that romance and relationships do not need to be the main storyline but rather are used frequently as a subplot.

Even non-fiction needs this development of relationships. If you are writing about clients who are attempting to lose weight, are they married or involved with someone or do they want to be involved with someone? Your reader will care more about these people you are using as examples in your weight loss book if they know them as real human beings with real lives including real relationships. If writing about investing, is this person married, and do they always agree on their investments? If writing about your favorite recipe from your Grandmother, why not include the story of how your grandparents met and married?

Again, to create romance and relationships you will start on page one and read your entire manuscript concentrating on where you can add these personal feelings to your story. This will also be your third rewrite.

I hope you are beginning to see how you are building your book one layer at a time. It is much easier to concentrate on just one element that needs to be in a book at a time rather than trying to remember to put everything in your book all at once. And for all of you who panicked when told to write your book in just ten days, you should realize now that was just to get the story down on paper and then you go back and rewrite several times to catch all the mistakes and change things around.

NOTE: Does your favorite movie have any romance or strong relationships in it?

This step should also take about two to four days.

However, no matter how serious your subject matter, you need to bring a smile to your reader. If your reader is depressed by the end of your book, they will not want to read your next book.

8. Creating Comic Relief

It's time to add another element, and an extremely important one, to your book. The Greeks were famous for their tragedies but Shakespeare was the one who made a science of this. Up until Shakespeare's time, all playwrights were niche writers because, if they wrote a tragedy it was really tragic, if they wrote about royalty it was totally about royalty, if they wrote a comedy it was completely comedy. Shakespeare did the same thing until he discovered that, if he wrote a love story, only people who liked love stories would show up to watch. But that did not fill all the seats. He quickly discovered that he needed to have something for everyone in each of his plays in order to fill all the seats in his audience. You need to have something for everyone in order to sell all your books. Therefore, you need well developed characters, at least some dialogue, at least some action/adventure, and some kind of romance/relationships, as well as comedy in each book you write in order to appeal to all the readers. These are the basic elements of any good book or movie or TV show.

Many people are teaching writing classes today based on writing a niche book. They say that it is easier to sell a niche book. They are correct because for any book out there you will find at least a couple of magazines on that same subject. All you need to do is put a little ad in a couple of these magazines to advertise it directly to people interested in your subject. The problem with this method of writing is that those little ads will cost several thousand dollars each month! It is much easier and more cost effective to have something for every reader in your book.

Comedy is very important for several reasons. For one thing, if you are writing a very serious book you need something light to break up the seriousness. For instance, if you are writing about the death process, you need to add a few light moments but that refer to what you are writing about. One woman told me about her husband's bout with cancer. After he passed away, at his request, she had a dinner for all his friends at a restaurant looking out on the ocean where they could all see his ashes being disbursed at sea. The dinner was filled with people talking about what they remembered about him including a lot of funny stories. Everyone was laughing and enjoying their memories. As people were leaving, a woman from across the restaurant came up to her to comment on what a wonderful party they had had and asked what the occasion was. The hostess, with a big smile, said, "Oh, my husband died." Needless to say, at the time she was embarrassed by how she had said that but later realized that it was a funny way to show what is needed during a time of grief.

Another very important reason to add a little comedy is that laughs sell! If you are writing a book that is completely comedy, it is very easy to sell. But all books need some humor. You will do the same thing you did with the previous steps. Start on page one and re-read your manuscript deciding where you can add a little (or a lot of) humor. Of course, this means you will also be doing your fourth rewrite.

Keep in mind that the most popular movies have all of these elements. Star Wars, Indiana Jones, Harry Potter, The Mummy all had action adventure, romance/relationships, and comedy.

There is a notion out there in the world that writing a niche book is easier to sell. Yes, I agree it is easier. After all, if you are writing a science fiction book, all you have to do is advertise it to people who read science fiction. You would do that by putting ads in the magazines that science fiction readers like. Easy, right? But very expensive! To put a small ad in the three cheapest scifi magazines each month would cost you around $6,000. So it is easier to sell niche books but extremely expensive! However, if you take that niche book and add all the different elements so that it has something that will appeal to everyone in the audience, it is much easier to sell.

This brings up another issue. I feel you need to decide (preferably before starting your manuscript) what you want to get from your book. That is, if you want to write the great American novel that wins all the awards and critical acclaim, than go for it. However, which is more important to you personally: winning the awards or writing a very popular book that people will be reading for generations to come. Unfortunately, at least in this country, those two things do not go together. The ones that win all the awards and get the critical acclaim are not the ones popular with everyone. For instance, I have asked in my classes what movie won the Oscar last year and usually I can find one person who will remember the name of that movie. However, when I ask people to raise their hands if they ever watched it, I am lucky if three people out of 30 ever bothered to see it. I wish things were different but, since they are not, you need to decide whether you want to write an award winner or a popular book.

You should allow about two to four days and to add the comedy and for the fourth rewrite.

By now, having added all of these essential elements to your book and having rewritten it four times, you should have caught all the changes and errors possible, keeping in mind that there is no such thing as a perfect book or a perfect writer. But there are a few other things we need to check in this book before it is ready to print.

9. The Final Rewrite

As you added each element, you did another rewrite wherein you corrected and changed things. But this is the big rewrite! At this point, you can either work off of your computer or you can print out your manuscript. Starting on page one, you will read the first sentence either to yourself or out loud (whichever works best for you). Then you need to ask yourself, "How can I make this sentence better?" Then you read the second sentence and ask yourself how you can make it better. And then the third sentence. Now you read the whole paragraph together and ask yourself how you can make it better. You will be doing this all the way through your book, one sentence at a time, one paragraph at a time. Yes, this is very time consuming and picky work.

However, there is one more thing you need to do at the same time and that is check for spelling, punctuation and grammar. Please keep in mind that studying English and writing a book are two different things.

If you are not sure of the use of a word or its spelling, you need to use the good old-fashioned dictionary. Your computer spell check will not work for this.

You need to decide which form of punctuation you want to use in your book and you need to decide before it ever goes to an editor. For whatever reason, there are several forms of punctuation. You need to go to the library and skim a few books on punctuation to decide which method is the most comfortable for you to use. If you need to, buy a copy of that to keep on your desk for reference.

Writers use a lot of literary license when it comes to grammar. If you are telling someone a story, you have a lot of things you can use to get the story across to your listener. You have your voice and its inflections, you have facial expressions and body movement, and you may even act out some parts. However, when writing a book, you have a piece of white paper with black ink. So how can you get across all the nuances? I will do things such as start sentences with the word "and" or "but", terrible grammar mistakes. But if that is what I have to do (as with this sentence) to show that this is important, then that is what I will do. In order to catch the reader's attention, you might write something like, "Then there was Tom. Thirty-five years old. Went in for a physical. Told he has six months to live." In other words, we may not even use complete sentences in order to create more drama.

As this step takes a lot of patience and care, you should allow about 5 to 10 days for it.

At this point you should have caught all changes, typos, etc. that it is possible for you to find. Now there is just one more simple step before sending this manuscript to the printer.

10. The Final Reading

At this point I recommend you print your manuscript out on 8 ½ x 11 inch paper and double spaced. Now find your favorite reading spot and read this book from beginning to end. Keep in mind that you are not reading *your* book but *this* book, as though you just picked it up at the library. You have already made all the changes and corrections you can so just relax and read. At some point you should find yourself thinking, "This is a good book! I like it!" This is not an egotistical statement. This is simply a reader who is enjoying a good book. You know you have thought this to yourself before when reading some book. Now you know your book is ready to print.

However, there are a few of you who are perfectionists. You know who you are. You can read your manuscript for years and still feel it is not quite right, there's something wrong with it. You don't know what it is, you just know you are not happy with it. Therefore, that poor book will never see the light of day.

However, there is a cure for perfectionists - - you follow the previous 9 steps and do the very best you can and now you PRINT your book. If you must, then just blame me! "I have to print my book because Bobbie said so!"

This means you will have to live the rest of your life with a book you are unhappy with, right? Wrong!

28

If you have written a non-fiction, it is extremely common, even mandatory, to rewrite your book every 2 to 3 years and bring it out as a "new, updated version". After all, numbers and statistics change over a couple of years. Or you have used different people for examples of what you are trying to teach others. So what if during the last 2 or 3 years since your book came out you met someone else who had a great story and you wish you had known about it before you wrote your book. No problem. You will just rewrite your book using the new examples and issue a new edition. Actually, issuing new editions is very good for sales.

But what if you have written a work of fiction? Again, it is very common today with the best selling authors to rewrite a story. For instance, you read a "new" book and find yourself in one or two places thinking this sounds familiar, like you have read it before. Then you get to the end of the book and, across from the last page, it says "Author's note - This book was originally published five years ago but I was never quite happy with it. So I have changed some of the story and added a couple of new characters. Hope you enjoy it."

Again, this is very common today. Even if you have printed your story and not felt totally comfortable with it, at some point in time you will find yourself thinking, "That's what I should have done!" So, when you are approaching the end of the run, you just rewrite your work of fiction and issue it as a new book. However, I would suggest putting the "Author's Note" at the beginning of the story rather than the end. Anyone who likes your books will read this one because you have told them you have changed parts of it and anyone who has never read your work before will enjoy it as a brand new story.

These are the only 10 steps you need to follow in order to complete your manuscript. Hopefully you see by now that it is much easier to concentrate on just one aspect of your book at a time rather than trying to writing a complete book all at once. However, there is one more thing you need to consider.

Getting A Copyright

If you will be sending your manuscript to publishers, you will need to fill out a Form TX copyright form. You can go to www.copyright.gov or call them at 202-707-3000. Keep in mind that you cannot copyright the title of your book or the ideas in your book. You can only copyright verbatim what you have written. Unfortunately this is not a lot of protection. It is not at all uncommon for a publisher to receive a manuscript, like it, and take it to one of his in-house writers to write this book. So long as the wording is different, this is legal. He can even use your title. However, as the copyright is the only protection you have, I suggest you fill it out and send it in.

Keep in mind that the old notion of sending yourself a certified copy of your manuscript does not usually hold up in court these days.

If you will be self-publishing, you might not bother with a copyright. You will see your manuscript, an editor will see it, and you might have a couple of friends read your book. Let's pretend that one of your friends or the editor reads your manuscript and says to himself, "Wow! This is a great book. I think I'll steal it." So he puts his name on the title page and gets a copyright on your work in January. Now you do not know about this happening so you blissfully go on your way and get your book into print in June. Who owns this book? You do. Every time this goes into court the print date stands up over the copyright date so it is a matter of who got it into print first. However, if he got the copyright in January and then printed the book in March and you did not print till June, then he owns the book.

We have been talking about copyright as it applies to your work. However, you also need to think of how it applies to other writers.

The general rule of thumb (although not the law) is if you are quoting no more then two sentences from another author and you give them complete footnote credit for that quote, this is usually acceptable. However, if you are quoting more then those two sentences, you will need to get the owner's permission in writing. To contact the owner, or to find out who actually has the copyright on this material, contact the publisher of the magazine, book, show or wherever you found this quote. They will know who owns the rights to it.

If you are using photographs in your book, keep in mind that you must get permission from the person who owns the old run-down barn that you thought was so picturesque before using it for a commercial purpose (selling a book is a commercial purpose). Also remember that just because a monument or building is on Federal land (land that you and I own as citizens) does not mean you can use a picture of it without getting permission. That monument might be owned by the government and thus you can use it. But it could be owned by the designer/architect, the builder/sculptor, or the organization that commissioned the building or statue and you will need to get written permission.

If you are using any song titles or lyrics in your book, remember that you must get written permission to use that and you will probably have to pay the owner (the writer, performer, or producer) a royalty for each copy sold of your book or a flat fee. Music people are very protective of their copyrights.

These are just some general rules concerning copyright. If you are concerned about the material you are using, you should contact a lawyer.

Some Closing Thoughts

Always remember that this book you are writing is yours. If you want others to read it, it must be a work of entertainment. If it is a fiction, people want to be entertained by it. If it is non-fiction, others will learn what you are trying to teach them if you do it in an entertaining way. There is no reason for even a text book to be dull and boring today. Reading a book should be like spending the evening with a good movie or TV show. How long will you watch a dull movie? How long will you watch a boring cooking show?

After completing these 10 steps you should have a book about 250 pages long. Fiction readers today expect a story to be about 250 to 350 pages. Non-fiction readers (usually not as avid readers) will only have the patience for a maximum of 250 pages. However, even if your manuscript is less then 250 pages, don't worry about it. A trend in the last few years has been to combine two or even three short works of fiction into one book. This works particularly well when the second story is based on one of the secondary characters from the first story or if both have the same theme (Christmas, a particular town, the same detective, all about cats, etc.). If you are still worried about the length of your story, remember that each written page usually equals about one minute on film.

An important part of your marketing is naming your book. As soon as you know in your heart and soul that you are going to finish this book and get it into print, you need to start thinking of yourself as a writer. From that moment on when someone asks you what you do, I do not want to hear that you are a secretary (or whatever). From the time you decide to actually complete your book, you are now a writer and you need to let people know. So when you tell someone you are a writer, what is the first thing they ask you? "What are you writing?" Therefore, you need to have a title ready to tell them in order to start selling your book.

The most important thing to keep in mind concerning your title is this: The title must tell the reader what the book is about. For instance, I recently saw a book entitled "Flame in The Dark." What is this book about? No one knows! You need to figure out what is the most important thing you want people to learn from your book (non-fiction) or what this book is really about (fiction) and get that into the title. As most bookstores and libraries have computer systems allowing only 30 or 45 characters for the book title (they do not list sub-titles), you need to get the most important thing within the first few words. No book should ever start with "how to" because you can tell the reader what your book is about without using "how to". For instance, "How to Build Your Garden" can just as easily be called "Garden Building".

Read the types of books you want to read and read a lot of them. You will learn how you want to sound from the good writers and learn what not to do from the poor writers.

Every character and scene in your book must have a problem to solve. In fiction, you create a page-turner by having a new problem come up in each chapter. In non-fiction, each chapter will talk about a particular problem and how to solve it but still have that cliff-hanger in the final paragraph to keep the reader reading.

Write so you can see your story in your head. This will make it much easier to get the interest of a theatrical agent who can sell your book to a movie or TV producer.

Every book needs all the same elements to keep the reader absorbed – action/adventure, romance/relationships, comedy.

Stick to your calendar. In the next section on publishing you will see why this is so important.

If you are doing a biography or autobiography, I highly suggest doing it as a fiction in order to get more exposure in the fiction section of the library and bookstore and to allow yourself more literary license.

Keep a file of story ideas in case you get stuck half way through your book. Just glancing through all your ideas might help you add a new character that will get your book going again. Or perhaps you see an idea that would make a good sub-plot in your book. If you really feel you cannot finish this book, the best cure is to get your mind totally off of it. Do this by taking one of your ideas and start a new book.

I think a writer should enjoy writing. If you are making yourself miserable forcing yourself to go into that office every day and trying to write something, then maybe you are not a writer. If so, accept that fact and move on to trying one of the other thousands of things out there you can do.

You are writing a book because you either have a story that you want to entertain people with or because you want to teach people something or, if you are really good, you will entertain and teach in the same book. Enjoy your work.

Now that you have your manuscript ready to print, you need to learn about publishing and marketing your book. I highly suggest that you work on the publishing and marketing of your book while you are still writing it. I fully realize how difficult writing a first book is, but you will find in the coming sections that it will help you tremendously (particularly financially) if you can work on the other two parts while you are still writing. If you have ever dreamed of becoming a full-time writer, you will need to bring in money and keep it coming in to stay in business. No matter how much you love what you are doing, the fact of life is that you still need to make a living. You will see in the marketing section that you can actually sell copies of your book before you have even finished writing it which will help pay for the publishing.

PART II – Publishing Your Book

In this section we will talk about several things, most important of which are how to sell your work to a publisher and how to self-publish. The only way you can decide what course to take is if you have all the information about each method first. However, we will be covering other topics such as freelance writing, POD, ebooks, etc.

Freelance Writing

A lot of writers, including myself, get started in the writing business by doing freelance writing or writing articles and/or short stories for magazines. If you are unknown, you will find that sending query letters (as suggested in so many books on writing today) is a waste of time. I have found two methods for getting into freelance work that work very well.

On is to do a story you are interested in and submit it to magazines using the Writer's Market for Publications. However, this can be frustrating. An easier method is to check your Sunday newspaper each week under the jobs listings. As these are alphabetical, look under "writers". Every so often you will find an ad looking for a full-time or part-time writer in the technical field or commercial field. Contact these people but explain that you are a freelance writer. Most of these places would prefer to work with freelancers to avoid payroll costs. Once you get an assignment the most important thing you must do in order to get repeat business and to be recommended to other publishers is to always meet your deadlines. Deadlines are the most important thing in publishing. If you already have something published to show them, you should be able to start at about $75 per article. You have to cover the costs of interviewing people and research.

Another way to start building your reputation and that will even look good on your cover letter to publishers is to write a story/article and offer it to small newspapers (non-union) and magazines for free. That is, at least you will get published and no one else need know that you did not receive any pay for it.

How to submit your work to a publisher

First of all, do not waste your time with a literary agent for several reasons. One, if you do manage to get an agent he will be collecting 10% of what you make for the rest of your life. Two, a lot of them say they will represent you if you pay them a couple hundred dollars for a professional critique of your book first. A good agent never does this. Three, of the thousands of writers I have worked with over the years, none have gotten into print using an agent. However, we have had three authors who self-published, worked hard at marketing, and then sold the movie rights to their book through a theatrical agent.

To sell your work to a publisher you will first need a copy of the Writer's Market which is available at any library or bookstore. This lists all publishers by topic area. If you have written a fiction or non-fiction, you will submit the first two chapters of your book along with a one-page cover letter. If you are doing a children's book, submit the whole story but without any pictures along with a one-page cover letter. Unfortunately, most publishers prefer to have their own in-house artists do the graphics for children's books.

The letter's first sentence and only the first sentence must tell why your book is so special or different from every other book. Use one more sentence to tell what you have already had published and any awards you have won. The rest of the cover letter must explain your marketing plan in detail for the first 30 days your book is out. Keep in mind that you only have 30 days in which to sell all of the books printed. After 30 days all remaining books will be returned to the publisher to make room for all the new books coming out next month. Your marketing plan will be discussed in the next section. You will also tell the publisher how much money you are planning on spending for the marketing. This is not money that you give to the publisher but what you will use yourself to do the marketing. Basically, the publisher wants to see that you are willing to put your time and effort and money into selling your book because there are three guaranteed things in life – taxes, death, and the only person who can sell your book is you the author. Publishers are very well aware that they cannot sell your book and if you are not willing to do the marketing then why should they publish it?

As you are probably already aware, the chances of finding a publisher for your book are extremely slight and those that are usually from established writers or celebrity writers.

If a publisher does decide to buy your book, as a new unknown writer you will receive about 2% to 4% royalties (from the cover or retail price) on each book actually sold to the public. IMPORTANT: A book is NOT sold when it goes into a bookstore. It is only sold when someone from the public comes in and buys that book.

Therefore, if your book retails for $15.00 and you find a generous publisher who gives you 5%, you will make 75 cents from each book sold. Also be aware that if a publisher gives you any upfront money (this very seldom happens), it is only a lone to you. They will repay this upfront loan to you from your royalties. If you do not sell enough books to pay back the advance, you still owe them this money.

However, please do not be discouraged by all of this. Remember that about 80% of all books you see in any bookstore today are self-published. It's easy, it's inexpensive, and you get to keep all the profits from your hard work.

Self-Publishing

If you feel very strongly about your work, you can join the 80,000+ self-published authors in this country and produce your own book. Mark Twain was self-published. However, in his day, it cost a lot to self-publish. Today, thanks to the desk top computer, it is easy and inexpensive to start your own publishing company.

If you decide to self-publish, the smallest amount you will make from the sale of your book is 45% (those sold through bookstores). When we get into the marketing you will see that eventually most of your sales will be direct to the public meaning you will keep the entire retail amount, but when you are starting out with bookstores you do not make as much. This means if your book retails for $15.00, you will make $6.75 for each book sold. You can already see the difference in profit between selling to a publisher and self-publishing.

Publishing your own book is like having a baby in that there are certain steps you have to go through to insure a successful publication. However, you will be raising that child (marketing your book) for the rest of your life. If you sell your work to a publisher, you have 30 days in which to sell your books and then the stores are on to the new books this month. When you self-publish, you can keep selling that book forever. Again, remember that only you can sell your book. A publisher cannot do it for your, a bookstore cannot sell your book for you, it is up to you to let the public know about your great new book.

As stated before, once you have decided you are definitely going to finish your book and get it in print, you should start working on the publishing. Following are 11 steps to self-publishing. However, 2 of these are not necessary so you will actually be doing just 9 steps. Half of these steps are required even if you sell your work to a publisher and these will be pointed out to you.

1. Editor - Even if you sell your work to a publisher, you are responsible for hiring the editor. If you have ever read a book with typos on every page, it means that author did not realize they were responsible for the editing. The main reason that publishers do not handle editing is that they have been losing money on books for many years to the point where there are fewer and fewer large publishers. When a company is losing money, it must cuts costs somewhere and the easiest thing to cut is the editing. An editor will be checking spelling, punctuation, grammar and the flow of the work.

To find an editor you can go into your yellow pages and find professionals that charge from $50 to $100 per page or a set rate of about $1,500 for the entire book. However, it does not need to cost this much. Try advertising in your local college or university student newspaper for "a senior or graduate English student to edit books." The benefit of hiring a student is that it costs a lot less. Usually you can get a whole book done for $200 to $300. If hired, they will get credit on the title page of your book and get a finished copy when your book is printed for their portfolio.

2. Graphic Designer – If you sell your work to a publisher, they will use their own in-house graphic designers. If self-publishing, you will need to find one. This is someone who can do interior work, which we will talk about later, and design your book cover and computerize it for the printer.

Again, you can check your yellow pages keeping in mind that professionals will charge about $1,500 for a cover. You can also check to see if any of your colleges/universities have graphic design schools. A senior student should already have done sample book covers and know what to do. Again a student will probably charge about $400 for a cover.

We also recommend Mustang Graphic Designers for cover and/or interior work. They have worked with many of our students with excellent results. They charge about $500 for a basic book cover design (be sure to say, "Bobbie referred me to you"). You can contact them at 916 422-7109 or email them at MustangGraphic@aol.com. Or check them out at MustangGFX.com.

3. Printer – If you sell your work to a publisher, they will do the printing. For the self-publisher, printing is your biggest expense. You should get bids from at least three printers to compare service and price. Although it is very nice to support your local printers, you will find that they charge about double what the big Midwest printers charge because so much of their work has to be subcontracted out. These large printers specialize in small to medium publishers and have the capability to do everything in house thus saving you a lot of money. The following recommendations have been around for many years and should give you the best rates if you contact the person listed and say that Bobbie Christensen recommended you. That is, they will give good rates in order to get repeat business from the people I deal with. However, I personally have never had a book printed by the last one as of this date.

~~Central Plains Book Mgf., Sudie White, 877-278-2726~~
✓ good Sheridan Books, Kathy Brown, 734-475-9145
Thomson-Shore, Inc., Maria Smith, 734-426-1722

You will need to give them certain information so that when you get the bids you will be comparing apples with apples as follows:

a. Only get 1,000 printed. This may seem like a small amount until you are trying to sell them. If you ask for a bid for 1,000 and for 3,000, you will find that the cost per book is less if you go with the larger amount. However, once a printer has done your book, you have sold them all, and you call them for a reprint of another 1,000, you will find the reprint cost per book will be lower then the original cost for 3,000 because they have already done the setup work.

POD - This is a good time to mention POD (print on demand) printers also. Virtually every printer in the country will do POD of books. However, the cost is prohibitive. For instance, using one of my own books as an example, if I had 200 of them printed POD, I will get bids of from $5 per book to $19 per book (an average of $10 per book). That means you will spend $2,000 for just 200 books. Keep this mind when you read further to how much normal printing should cost.

b. You will want a soft cover rather than hard cover. A hard cover will cost you a great deal more and you have to keep in mind that the reading public does not want to pay for the high cost of hard bound books. Today even libraries have no problem ordering good soft cover books.

You will also need to tell them the weight of the cover which is only .01 weight. You can get much heavier if you are concerned and wanted a hard cover. Go into your local college book store and you will see that most text books today are soft cover with heavier stock and special coatings to protect them. This would still be more economical then going with a hard cover.

c. You will need to tell them the finished size of your book. My books are all 5 ½" x 8 ½", a very standard size today. If you will be doing an unusual size for a cook book or children's book, you will need to tell them what the size is you want. However, if that is not one of their standard sizes, you will pay more for that unusual size. Therefore, ask them if this is one of their standard sizes and, if they say no, ask them for the next nearest standard size. This might be another ½" larger then what you wanted but it will save you money.

d. You need to tell them the weight of the interior paper which is usually 60 pound white. Going with anything thinner could cause bleed-throughs. If you are doing something with photography in it, you might need a heavier paper, however, please read on about what to do if your book has color in it.

e. You will need to tell them how many pages your manuscript will be. If you are doing as you should and thus working on the publishing before you have even finished writing your book, you will have to guess. Just give them a round number like 250, 300, 350. When you actually accept one of the printers and send in your manuscript, they will send you a revised bid showing what the cost was for the original number and what the cost is for the new number of pages.

f. If you need to have interior layout done and you want the printer to do it, you will need to let them know now as it will make a big difference in the bid you get back. Most books do not need interior layout because they are black print and nothing else. If you do need to have photos, charts, etc. put into your print, I would recommend doing it yourself if you are computer literate enough to do it. If you are not computer literate (as I am not), I recommend having your graphic designer do it for you. They will usually give you a big discount as they are already doing the cover for you. The last choice would be to have your printer to it as they will charge a lot more for that work.

g. Will the cover be 2-color or full-color? Full-color will cost from $200 to $400 more then the 2-color cover. Keep in mind that a good graphic designer can do a lot with just 2 colors. As white is the color of the cover stock, you get white for free. You also get all the variations in shades of those two colors.

h. Your book will need some sort of coating to protect the ink in shipping. This only adds a couple of cents in cost to each book but is worth it.

i. You will want a perfect bound book although most large printers today are offering notched perfect bound which will hold together better. If you are doing a cook book or a work book that you want a person to be able to open up and have it stay open, you want to ask for a lay flat perfect bound. It looks exactly the same but when you open the book it stays there. Stay away from spiral binding as it costs a lot more and is extremely difficult to get into libraries and book stores.

j. You will need to give them the date they will receive your manuscript. You may remember that we said in the first section on writing that you need to keep a calendar and put the completion date on it. This is very important. When you sign your contract the printer will put you in their calendar for that date. If the printer does not receive your manuscript on the date they expect it, they will assume you did not write your book and cross you off their calendar. Then when they do receive it a few days late, you are put at the bottom which can create a huge delay for you. The usual turn around time for a first time print should be about 4 to 5 weeks (unless you are trying to get it printed during the holiday season of October through December). If they put you at the bottom, you will be lucky to see your book in three months. In other words, when you do get behind, update your own calendar and call the printer to let them know. They will keep updating their calendar so long as you keep them informed.

From these things the printer will send you a bid. You will sign a contract to tie into that price. Now you need to submit your manuscript.

Today the usual submission method is electronic. You will need to ask your printer exactly how they want it submitted. Because things can go wrong between your computer and their computer, I highly recommend paying for a proof. This is one print they will send you to see if everything looks okay. Keep in mind that it is not a guarantee that everything will go correctly with the printing but it takes care of most problems. Your graphic designer will submit the cover to the printer for you and will get a proof of the cover also.

Unless you are having someone do interior layout for you, you will actually to the "type setting" yourself on your computer. Although you usually write a manuscript double-spaced on 8 1/2" x 11", you will need to reformat it to fit the size book you want. For instance, if you want the finished size to be 5 ½" x 8 ½", you will need to take out the double spacing and bring in the left and right margins to fit your book. I always leave a 1" margin at the top and left side and want the same for the bottom and right side so I bring in the right and bottom to 3.5" (under file click on page setup).

You may have noticed that this book is done in larger then normal size print. It is 12 point. You might also notice that this book (and all my other books) is much thinner then other books. I have a reason for this. Over 10 years ago I wrote my first book, "Getting A Free Education". Because it was meant for people who would never have the opportunity to go to college, I wrote it at a 9th grade reading level with large print and only 128 pages. It was important to me that people get this information. However, I found that from the first day of sales to the last, the majority of people who bought this book already had a Masters or Ph.D. but they would say, "Easy to read. I like that!"

Unfortunately we are dealing with a non-reading public. That is only about 50% of our adult population every buys even one book a year. Because of this I decided to make all my books (including my mysteries) short and to the point and with larger print. This has worked out very well for me. However, that is only what I have done. It is up to you to decide what you want from your book.

What does all this printing cost? For a book similar to what you are holding in your hand, you should get a bid of about $2.20 per book or $2,200. Obviously, a larger book will cost more but should not reach $3.00 per book. This is the largest cost when you self-publish. If you are doing a book with full color inside (color photos or children's book), the only way to keep the printing affordable is to go to a Hong

Kong printer. For this you need a Hong Kong agent. We recommend Tim Flynn at 916-985-~~9696~~ 4471 or tim@flynnandflynn.com. In order to get a decent price you will need to have at least 2,000 printed. For the average 28-page, full-color children's book (stapled spine), this should run you about $3.00 per book or a total of $6,000.

Do not despair! I realize this is a lot of money to you but there are solutions. For instance, if you do not know where you can come up with $2,000 to get your book printed, please read the marketing section of this book wherein we explain how to sell copies of your book before you have even finished writing it. If you are doing a full-color interior book, use your imagination and think of how you can do your book without color. Instead of having full-color drawings in your children's book, could you change it into black outlines with the story at the bottom of each page and turn it into a coloring book (just two colors for the cover and a black interior would make this very affordable). Could you change the full-color pictures to sepia tones making it a two-color interior? Have your graphic designer change your cook book photos to black and white and cut your cost in half. Look at the best-selling cook book from Better Homes & Gardens that has only 10 or 12 full color pages in it.

If you are considering full-color interior, please go to the book store or library and pick up a copy of a Harry Potter book and glance through it. You will find that each chapter has a black pen-and-ink drawing at the beginning and no color at all. Yet these are best-selling books. You can capture a child's imagination and entertain them without color!

Again, look at what the POD book cost earlier. For 200 books printed POD, you are talking about $2,000. By doing the normal printing, you will be paying about $2,200 for

1,000 books! And, when you sell all 1,000 and need another thousand, they will cost even less.

We are not finished quite yet. There are still a few more things you need to do before you can get your book printed.

4. ISBN – If you are going to self-publish, you need to get your ISBN (International Standard Book Numbering). Go online to www.isbn.org to get the form or call them at 877-310-7333 (R. R. Bowker Data Collection Center). You will be filling this form out to establish yourself as a publisher (you are self-publishing). This form is submitted with about $225.

When you send this in you will get a list of ten ISBN's. As each new book (not reprints) will need a new ISBN, this is enough to do 10 different books and the list is good as long as you are alive for your self-publishing company. They will also provide you with directions and/or the form to list the current book you are working on wherein you will assign it one of the ISBN's. This gets your book into books in print which means anyone can go to any book store or library to find out how to purchase your book.

5. Library of Congress number – The Library of Congress actually has different number systems depending on whether you are a publisher or a self-publisher. Because this can cause discrimination against you as a self-publisher, we do not recommend getting either. In the old day no library would accept your book unless it was listed with the Library. However, libraries figured out a long time ago that if a customer wants that book, they will just order it using the ISBN. This is one of those steps that are not necessary. If you do want to list it with the library, go online to the Library of Congress for the forms.

6. Retail Price – If you sell your work to a publisher, he will set the retail price (selling price) of your book. If you self-publish, you will do this. There are many theories out there on how to set the price such five times or eight times the cost of publishing. It is more important to price according to the type of book you have written, fiction or non-fiction.

For a work of fiction or a children's book, it is difficult to go any higher than $12.95 because you are up against the big publishers that sell a paperback novel or a children's book for $6.50. However, because you will be selling the content of your book (see marketing section) you can go as high as $12.95. However, keep in mind that as you build your reputation with future books and good sales, you can start charging more per book.

With non-fiction you have a lot more leeway. Go into any bookstore and check what a book of your genre is selling for. You might find self-help books priced from $12.95 to $39.95. However, you need to keep in mind what the public is willing to pay. The majority of people will buy the book priced at $19.95 instead of the $39.95 book.

The method I use for my non-fiction books is to calculate just the printing cost of each book and then round that up to the next nearest dollar. For instance, if your book costs $2.30 each to print, then round the total cost up to $3.00. If the cost was $2.90, I would round it up to $4.00. This rounding up usually covers all the additional costs involved if you have published correctly because all those other costs break down into pennies per book. You paid $225 for 10 ISBN's. However, that means you only spent $22.50 for this book. However, since you had 1,000 printed, you actually spent .0225 cents per book (just over 2 cents). Let's say you paid a graphic designer $700 for your book cover. For 1,000 books printed you paid 70 cents per book. However, assuming you work hard and sell a lot of books and must get a reprint for another 1,000 (using the same cove), you have now paid just 35 cents per book. In other words, all of these miscellaneous costs broken down per book come to very little compared with the actual printing cost.

Personally, I do not recommend going over $19.95 for any book at this time as going to $20.95 causes a psychological problem. If you have decided you really want to buy a particular book and you ask how must it cost, you will be willing to pay $19.95. However, if you are told it cost $20.95 (or more), your brain automatically says, "Oh, over $20! That's a lot." It is better to sell books at a smaller profit then to not sell any books.

However, there is an exception to this rule. If you have written a truly one of a kind book, you can charge more for it. For instance, a woman in Chicago wrote a book on nail technology (doing finger nails). She decided to write it because, having been in the business for years, she had seen all of the problems involved in the business from people who did not sterilize their equipment to consumer's that had to have a finger amputated. Because there was no other book like this anywhere, she can easily charge $26.00 per book and sell a lot of books at that price.

7. Bar Code – Before you can print your book you need a bar code. The bar code will have your ISBN and price on it. Today most graphic designers will take care of this for you. However, I would recommend that you have them break out the cost for the bar code on a separate line of your bid. They should be charging only about $35 to $45 for the bar code.

8. Fictitious Business Name Statement or DBA – As a self-publisher you will be starting your own publishing business. You will register your business name usually through your County Clerk's Office. Some states have other offices for this but, if you contact your County Clerk's Office, they will tell you who to contact. You should also get this even if you are selling your work to a publisher to avoid conflict with other authors in your state using "your" name. For instance, if another writer goes by Jane Smith, you might need to add your middle initial or name in order to have your business registered.

9. Seller's Permit – You will get this permit through your County Franchise Tax Board or contact your County Clerk to find out where to get this. The seller's permit means you are registering your business so you will pay sales tax. I realize you would rather not do this but it is very important because it will save you money. When you send your manuscript to a printer they must also receive your seller's permit number or you will have to pay the sales tax for printing your books. As books are considered for resale (the end seller is usually a book store), the store will charge the customer sales tax. However, you will be responsible for the sales tax on any books sold in your state. The Board will send you a form monthly or annually on which you will state what you sold directly to the public and pay the sales tax on those sales.

10. Business License – You may need a city and/or county business license. The main purpose of these seems to be to generate more revenue for the government.

11. Bookkeeping – You just want to be a writer! Unfortunately, writing is also a business. However, as with any small business, the bookkeeping does not have to be overwhelming for us non-accountant types.

I recommend that you start your writing and/or self-publishing business as a Sole Proprietorship and keep it that way. Incorporating your company will just causes a lot more headaches with the government. I also highly recommend that you find a good accountant who has worked with other writers and understands the laws pertaining to this work. An accountant doing your taxes each year will cost you more money but will save you a lot of money in the long run.

In order for the accountant to do your taxes (and to keep the IRS happy) there is some bookkeeping you need to do. I recommend the two file folder method. You will have one file folder marked "income" and one marked "expenses".

You can create a work sheet on your computer that you can then copy. I call it my Daily Worksheet. I use one for each day I am working. At the top is a place for the location (what city or store I am in that day), the date, and what I am doing (seminar, book signing, etc.). Below that I keep track of the attendance (how many people were at the class or how many of which books I sold that day). Finally I list all sales as Cash, Checks, or Charges with a Total for the day.

If you are accepting charges (how to set this up is in the Book Signing section of Marketing) you will need a form containing the customer's name, address, phone number, what they are buying, the total cost of that purchase, their charge card number, its expiration date, and a place for them to sign the form. You can also purchase the small forms you have seen at stores but it is cheaper to make your own. You can also get the charge machine that prints out the form for the customer to sign but, since most class rooms and book stores will not have a place for you to connect to a phone line, you will need your own form. These forms will be kept in a separate file in case the IRS audits you. The total charges for the day will go on your daily worksheet.

If you accept checks, please make sure you make copies of all the checks before you deposit them. Unfortunately banks have been known to lose deposits. However, they can go ahead and credit all those checks if you have copies of them. The total dollar amount of those checks will be entered on your daily worksheet.

You will also keep track of how much you made in cash that day and enter it on your worksheet.

For your "Expenses" file, you will need to remember to get a receipt for anything and everything you buy and put all receipts in this folder. You do not need to separate them by date or by account. You simply need these in case the IRS audits you. You will be using the file at the end of the year to add up and give your accountant the different dollar expenses for the year.

Now we have covered all the steps involved in publishing your book including a couple of unnecessary steps. However, there is another form of publishing.

Ebooks are ordered by email and sent to the customer by email. This will probably be the way books are sold in another 50 to 100 years because fewer and fewer people are reading books. However, today most readers would rather curl up in bed with a good book then with a computer. However, the main objection to ebooks is that you never know whether you will be paid for any books sold or not. Because these books are generating very few sales, most of the businesses involved in them do not last over five years. And because they are losing money, they have a tendency not to pay the authors. Personally, at this point in time, I cannot recommend ebooks.

Some of you may be feeling a little intimidated by now. You know no publisher will buy your book but you don't see how you can do all the things we talked about in order to self-publish. First, take a deep breath and relax. The only reason you are worried is because you have just tried to learn a whole new business in just a few pages of reading. Those pages seem intimidating but are actually very easy to do and can be accomplished very quickly. Actually doing these steps will take less time then it took you to read the whole thing. It's kind of like when you started a new job back 10 years ago and on the first day another person trained you. At the end of that day, you are thinking, "How can I go in there and actually do this tomorrow when I can't even remember what she said today?!" But you do go in to work the next day and you fumble through asking a lot of questions. Then, three months later you know that job inside and out and you are now bored with that same job because it's just the same thing day after day. It's the same thing with publishing a book. The publishing is as easy as doing 9 steps and they become boring but they are necessary.

You stared reading this book in order to become a writer. You thought you would just write that book and the world would make you a best seller. Now you have discovered that you have to get involved in the publishing also. Now it is going to get even worse because you have to sell your books. But again, don't panic. You are about to learn a new business (just like the publishing) that you probably have never done before. Keep in mind it is not as difficult as you think.

PART III – Marketing Your Book

If there is one thing I can guarantee you (other then death and taxes), it is that you are the only one who can market your book. A book store cannot sell your book, a publisher cannot, and a wholesaler or distributor cannot. After all, a book store manager cannot autograph your book and no one wants to listen to a publisher talk about your book. Even if you sell your manuscript to a publisher, they cannot sell your book because who wants a to listen to a publisher speak about your book, much less autograph it. You must do the marketing yourself otherwise you have just wasted your time writing a book that no one (other then your best friend) will ever read.

When you finish with the following 6 step marketing plan you will wonder how you can possibly do it all. Keep in mind that if I can do this, you can do it. We were not born writing books (unless you happen to be born into a family of writers). Just like the publishing, you are about to learn another new job. It is a little more difficult then publishing and it takes more time, but the rewards are worth it. If you feel the rewards are not worth it, that just means you are not a writer and it's time to try another profession. Either way you will have learned a great deal.

This 6 step marketing plan is the same one I use to sell thousands of books every year. The steps are done in order of importance with the first 4 steps being extremely important. If you are not willing to do those first 4 steps, you will not sell enough books to make it worthwhile. The last 2 steps are less important at this time but will add to your overall sales.

Marketing does not have to cost $2,000 a month (minimum monthly cost for a publicity firm). Most marketing can fit into your weekly household expenses. And keep in mind that you should be marketing your book before you have even finished writing it!

Here are some facts to keep in mind:

If you sell your work to a publisher, you have 30 days from the time your book goes into the stores in which to sell all of them (nationwide). After the 30 days is up, the stores must make room for the 4,000 new titles coming out next month. All of your books that did not sell will be shipped back to the publisher. These are called *returns*. Average book returns to publishers is 80% (although you will not have this problem if you follow this method). 80% returns will drive a large publisher out of business quickly, let alone a self-published author. This is the major reason we have so few large publishers left today.

According to the American Booksellers Association, 99% of all books fail. That is, they are not marketed and, therefore, no one buys them. If you follow the following steps, you will not be a failure as our success rates for people using these methods are over 60%. We have been keeping statistics over the past ten years and find that about half of our seminar attendees actually finish publishing their books. Of these, at least 60% are marketing their books successfully. This means they are making the amount of money they want to from their book. If you are willing to put in the time and effort necessary, you should be able to build up to $100,000+ a year in sales. This will take more than one year as sales build on themselves over the years. If you must work full-time, as most authors do in the beginning, remember that this only means it will take you longer to build up your sales, but they will grow. Remember that the number one thing that will most affect your sales is how much do you care about your book. You must really care about it in order to do the work involved.

The marketing in this section is based on my life as a full-time writer. However, I realize some of you have no desire to become full-time writers. If so, you will need to do at least the first 4 steps in order to make any sales at all. Always remember, as with any business, the more you do the more you make. But money is not the most important thing. The biggest gratification of all is when your readers send you a letter or email telling you how wonderful your book was, how much you entertained them, and then ask when your next book is coming out. Money cannot buy the feeling that these comments will give you.

Now let's look at how you will let the public know about your great new book.

1. Flyers

Contrary to popular belief (and after having personally spent a great deal of money to find out), the best flyer is on colored paper with black ink. All the tri-fold, glossy, multi-colored flyers will not sell your book. What is important is what the flyer says to people and making sure it is very easy to read. The next page is the sample flyer we will use (pretend it is on goldenrod paper).

Your flyer is the most important thing you will do in marketing and should be created while you are still writing your book. It will be used for everything you do including handing it out at book signings and seminars and mailing it to your reading list, libraries, the media, bookstores, etc. The following items *must* be on your flyer but not necessarily in the same order they are given.

A. A **catch phrase** in large bold lettering that can be read from 6 feet away is the most important thing. Less than 50% of our adult population ever buys even one book a year. That means we are dealing with a "non-reading" public (they are not illiterate but they do not enjoy reading). If they read this catch phrase and are not interested, your flyer ends up in the garbage so you better make it good. However, the biggest problem with creating a good catch line is that what you feel, as the author, is most important about your book may not be what the reader feels is most important. Therefore, you need to start with what you feel is the most important thing but realize it will probably change. For instance, on our sample, the original catch phrase read, "How to find safe, secure investments, growing 100% or more a year, and without using a stock broker." This is a good descriptive sentence that really tells what this book is about. However, when speaking directly to individuals at book signings, I found that when I

Building Your Financial Portfolio On $25 A Month (Or Less)
by Bobbie and Eric Christensen

Winner of the 1998 Best Business Book

Turn $25 a month into $100,000 in just 10 years, safely!

> *"...the best book I've ever seen for the small investor...a must read for even minimum wage earners...should be taught in every junior high school..."* (Manuel Carbahal, CPA, Davis, CA)
>
> *"Magnificent! It gives me real hope for the future. For the first time in many years I feel like I understand the stock market and the right way to go about investing."* (Tom Kay, Houston, TX)

Written for adults and teenagers in simple language explaining how you can build your financial portfolio SAFELY on as little as $5 a month!

- **Easy explanations and comparisons of: all types of mutual funds including Pension Plans, IRA's, 401K's, etc.; brokers and discount brokers; how the stock market and our economy work; and more.**

- **How to decide which investment is right for you with examples showing what your $25 a month can grow into in just 10 years.**

- **How to do the necessary research in just 15 minutes and track your investments for the IRS without becoming an expert.**

- **A 25 year proven method for protecting your future and save for a new home, education, retirement, or whatever is most important to you!**

The Christensen's are retired bankers who have been doing this type of investing for over 25 years. Bobbie has been a freelance writer for over 30 years with ten books published including the best-selling *Top 50 Best Stock Investments*.

978-0-9729173-2-2
$15.95

To order, call 1-800-929-7889 or go online to www.BooksAmerica.com

said, "If you had bought one share of General Electric 10 years ago and put $25 into that account every month for that 10 years, you would now have about $100,000," people would say, "Oh!" Whenever you say something that grabs people they will always say "Oh." When you hear that, you need to write that phrase down right away so you can change your flyer. So when you do finish your flyer, rather than print thousands of copies that may need to be changed quickly, only have 200 to 400 copies run which will be enough for two book signings and give you a chance to test out that flyer..

B. If you caught a person's attention with your catch phrase, they will now go to the top of the page. There we have the title of the book. It will be in smaller letters because the catch phrase is more important unless you have a title that really grabs people and tells exactly what your book is about.

C. Below that is the author's name in smaller letters. When you are famous, you can put your name in big letters. For now, don't waste the space.

D. Note the award this book has won. Some people prefer to list all of the awards their book wins on their flyer and all future printings of their book. Personally, I chose the award I like the best rather than list all of them. Remember that, once your book is in print, you are responsible for submitting it for awards. You can find a lot of these in writers' magazines.

E. There is a black and white rendition of the cover. People get a lot of flyers and, because they are usually non-readers, in order to know what this flyer is about they need a picture of the book because they don't want to read the whole flyer to find out what it is about.

F.   When your manuscript is completed (before printing) you want to submit copies to a couple of friends asking them to read your book and give you a review of it. However, as most people do not know how to write reviews, it is recommended that you have a one page review of your book that you have written placed on top of your manuscript. You can then ask them to write a review or, if they prefer, to use the one on top. You will use a couple of really good quotes from these people on your flyer.

G.   The next 2" provide your major selling points or why the customer should want your book. Please note that each sentence is no more than two lines with double spacing in between for easier reading.

H.   Finally you have a short paragraph about the author, then the ISBN, the price of the book, and where they can buy a copy.

This is your basic flyer that will be used for just about everything you do. However, when using this for a **library mailing**, you will put an additional line at the bottom saying, "Available from *name of distributor or wholesaler*". We will talk about distributors and wholesalers later. You can purchase a library mailing list for about $100 or simply spend a day at your library using their reference on libraries in the United States. The states and cities within them are alphabetical. Each library will have a short paragraph about it. Toward the end will be "new acquisitions" with a colon and dollar amount. This is how much the library is allowed to buy new books each year. You can pick out the libraries with the largest dollar amount and create a mailing list that you will use for many years to come.

As soon as you have decided to complete your book (print it), you need to start marketing it. The first obvious way is to tell your friends and co-workers about it. The usual response from these people will be something like, "Let me know when it comes out so I can get a copy." If you want to sell books, you don't let them get away that easily. You want to start a **mailing list** with the names and addresses of anyone who shows any interest as well as anyone who actually buys your book. This mailing list can go into your computer for ease in making mailing labels. You should do a mailing to everyone on your mailing list twice a year, once in the spring between February and May and once in the fall in October (for the holiday sales). You will be sending them your flyer. You do this in order to keep your book in their memory. That is, they may have read your book and loved it but next month they are reading a different book and loving it. Using your mailing list is a good "word of mouth" sales use. When that person who loved your book is reminded of it by receiving a flyer, they are more apt to think of buying another one for a friend or relative. I have had people receive my October flyer and order up to 20 copies as gifts for the holidays all for just the cost of a postage stamp. Also, when you have another book coming out, people who bought and loved your first book will be very easy sales. You can also do repeat mailings like this using postcards that are cheaper to produce and mail. However, keep in mind that you can't get much information on a postcard. Personally I have had much better response when using letter size mailings in an envelope then from using postcards.

A very important use of your flyer is for **Pre-Release Sales**. You need to start doing pre-release sales as soon as you are sure you are going to get your book into print. At the bottom of your flyer, you will create a small order form titled "Special Pre-Release Sale" that will say something like, "This book is due out in October 2007 for $14.95 plus $4 shipping and handling. **Buy it now for just $12.95 and free shipping**". In other words, you are offering a special deal if they buy the book now even though you have not finished writing your book yet. In other words, if you were worried in the last section on publishing how you could afford to get your book into print, these pre-release sales will generate money while you are still writing to use for the printing. I have covered from 40% to 200% of my printing costs using this method.

We will be talking about using your flyer for other things as we go along.

2. Book Signings

A book signing is the easiest, the cheapest, and the fastest way to get your book's name and your name out in front of the public. They are easy to set up, starting close to home makes them inexpensive, and you can be selling books within two weeks after they are printed. According to the ABA, during the average 2 hour book signing a total of 3 books will be sold. However, that is the national statistic and does not apply here. If you are willing to do the following, you will have a minimum of 20 to 30 sales per book signing (although we have authors reporting much higher sales using this method).

There are two things to consider: how to set up a book signing and how to do it so you sell a lot of books.

A. To set up book signings you will need your calendar and a list of where to give signings. In order to be a small success, you must plan on doing at least one event every week of the year (there are 52 weeks in the year). An event is a book signing, a speaking engagement, a radio interview, or something where you will sell books. Doing just one a week will not sell as many books as I do but at least you will be keeping your name out in front of the public so they don't completely forget about you.

You will also need a list of book stores in the area you want to cover. The easiest way to get this is to go online to the book store you are interested in and get a print out of their store locations along with phone numbers. Now you can pencil in when and where you want to do signings. Just keep in mind that the more you do, the more you will sell.

I will be using Waldenbooks as an example here for several reasons one being that thousands of people will walk past a Waldenbooks in a mall situation while only 200 to 300 will walk into a stand-alone Barnes and Noble on any given day.

You will need to set up book signings two months ahead of time to allow for media coverage. Following is a short script that you might want to practice before making any phone calls.

First you need to call and ask for the manager of the store. Personally I first ask what the manager's name is. When you get to speak with the manager, you will start with:

You: Hi. My name is Bobbie Christensen and I'm an author from Sacramento, California. I have a new book out called "Building Your Financial Portfolio On $25 A Month Or Less" that is selling great! *(Even if your book is not out yet, it is selling great)* I will be in your area and wondered if I could do a book signing with you on Thursday, April 25th from noon to 6:00? *(Another reason I prefer Waldens is that they will allow you to do a signing all day long whereas the others will only let you do a 2 hour signing. Obviously you can sell more books in 6 hours then you can in 2 hours).*

Manager: (may ask for ISBN or what your book is about or where they can get it and will then check their calendar. Give them whatever information they ask for)

You: (at some point in conversation) I will mail you a confirmation today that gives you all the ordering information you will need. I will also be contacting the media in your area and doing my own mailing for your area.

The managers love the fact that you will be contacting the media as they have no budget for it. It also tells them you are really going to work at selling your book.

You can easily create a confirmation letter on your computer that you can make copies of. Use letterhead and leave a space to hand write in the date you talked to the store, the name of the person you spoke with and their address, and the rest of the letter will be filling in the blanks. "This is to confirm that Bobbie Christensen agrees to do a book signing at (name of store) on (date) from (beginning time) to (ending time). You will then list the title and ISBN. Below that in larger letters put "Suggest ordering 10 copies". Even though you will be selling more, try to have them only order 10 copies. Then in very large bold lettering you will put "Available from *distributor or wholesaler*"

Before talking about how to do a good book signing, you need to know about some other very important facts.

B. First, what are **returns**? From the date your book goes into book stores you have 30 days in which to sell all of them. At the end of 30 days, the book store must make room for the 4,000 new titles coming in and will return any unsold books to the publisher. According to the ABA, for all authors today the average returns are 80%. If you have worked very hard to sell your book to a publisher and they get 80% returns, do you think they will want to publish your next book? And if you are self-published and get 80% returns, you will be out of business very quickly. I avoid returns by making sure that book only go into stores where I am doing a signing or in a store in a city where I will be giving a seminar. I do not try to get my books into every book store in the country because I have no way to market my books that widely. You would need at least a quarter of a million dollars for even a small nationwide marketing campaign in order to sell some of your books. Concentrate only on the areas you can do the marketing for.

This leads to the other important thing you need to know about. When you are starting out, book stores will not deal with you directly but must go through a middleman, that is a distributor or a wholesaler. You can do this in one of two ways.

Once your book is in print, you can submit it to a **distributor**. If they accept your book, they will send it out with their salespeople across the country trying to get every book store to carry your book. For this they take a 60% to 65% (or more) discount. That is, if your book retails for $19.95, they will keep that percentage in payment. I do not recommend using distributors because, again, do you have the money to sell those 30,000 books throughout the whole country? And if you cannot, then you end up with huge returns.

66

The other middleman is a **wholesaler.** They do not try to sell your book. You do. You set up a book signing with the store manager, the manager calls "special orders" at their home office to order your books, special orders contacts the wholesaler, the wholesaler contacts you, the publisher, to order the book. You ship the books to the wholesaler who ships them to the book store and the wholesaler is responsible for invoicing the book store and trying to do the collections (they must pay you whether they collect from the book store or not). For this, a wholesaler will take 55% to 60%. We highly recommend using Baker and Taylor, the largest wholesaler (although they are considered a distributor also) in the country (although they are currently owned by a Canadian company). Go online to Baker-Taylor.com for the forms. They require a 55% discount. You have to pay for their service but it is usually only one time. They charge this to set you up so stores can order your book but, once you have proven that you sell books, they usually do not charge for the listing of future books. Make sure you purchase only their basic service as the pricier one does no good.

Keep in mind that once you have proven that you sell a lot of books, most book stores will set you up with their own contracts to purchase directly from you. This can take a couple of years because the stores want to know that your marketing is an ongoing thing. Stores will contact you to deal directly with them when you have a running record of selling 20 to 40 books each and every month through that particular chain.

Now you need to do a good signing. Keep in mind that the average number of books old during a two hour signing is three! If you adhere to the following steps, you will sell a minimum of 20 to 30 books at each signing.

C. Two weeks before your book signing you need to call the manager to make sure they have your books in (or to remind them if they have not yet ordered them). On the day of your book signing you want to introduce yourself to the manager and remind them you are there to do your book signing. Another reason I like Waldenbooks is that they will put you at a table set right in the entrance to the store whereas the other stores will put you in a back corner. Also, Waldenbooks will let you do a book signing all day long if you are selling books whereas the others will only allow a two hour book signing.

They should have a table set up for you and you will want to borrow some of their book stands (or buy your own at any office supply store) to make a nice display with your books facing different ways so people can see them from any direction. Do not sit in the chair provide or you will be lucky if you sell three books. You will stand by your display with your flyers in one hand and one flyer always ready in your other hand. Any time you see someone glance toward you or your display you have to be ready to reach out with a flyer and ask, "Would you like information on my new book?" Keep in mind that you do not walk up to strangers and ask them what they are doing and neither will strangers just walk up to you. You have to be willing to reach out with a smile on your face.

There are 3 types of customers. One will say, "No thank you," so just go on to the next person. The second one will take a flyer and keep on walking. Carefully watch what these people do. If they are holding your flyer in front of their faces, chances are they are reading it. See if they come back to you. If they come back, you have a good flyer. If no one comes back, your flyer needs more work.

The third type of customer is my favorite. They take your flyer and stop right in front of you to read it. When they do, I think, "One thousand one, one thousand two," and then say, "Do you have any investments now such as a pension plan?" This will engage the customer in conversation and give you a chance to make them comfortable so they feel they can ask you questions and you can give them your 2 or 3 major selling points. Remember to smile and be happy because you are talking about your book (your baby)!

The most difficult thing to do in sales is the "close". This is when you actually asking the person to buy your book. What you will do is find a question that will work for you such as, "So, would you like an autographed copy today?" You are asking a question that requires them to make a decision. Maybe they say, "No, thank you." No problem, just start talking to the next person (personally I do not believe in using hard sales tactics). If they say yes, you will autograph the book for them, get them on your mailing list if possible, and send them to the clerk to pay for the book.

What if your customer tells you how much he would like your book but that he is unemployed and just can't afford it right now? What would you do? You hand him a flyer while pointing to your ISBN number at the bottom and tell him to take this flyer to the library, show the librarian this number, and "they will get the book for you for free". That customer now thinks you are wonderful because you are offering them your book for free at the library. However, keep in mind that when 2 people ask a library for a book, they order one copy.

What happens if you get to the book store and they tell you that your books did not come in time (or you just sold out of the 10 books they had gotten in the store)? If you are at a

Waldenbooks (Barnes & Noble and Borders will not do this and, if they do, you will not get paid for your sales), tell the manger, "No problem. I will bring in my own books from my car for display purposes only – I will not sell them – and take back orders for you." You want to have a back order form in your hand to show them. This is a sheet wherein you can write down the customer's name, address, phone number, and book ordered. This form is very easy to create on your computer and then just make copies of the original. "At the end of the signing, I will bring this list to you and you can call Baker & Taylor tomorrow morning to order just the books ordered. This way you won't have any returns." When you say "no returns", the manager will be happy to do this. Keep in mind that they will not let you sell your own books there.

You will also want to have a supply of "book plates" on hand. These are small, 2 ¾" x 4", colored plates. Find one with just enough room to sign your name. These can be found in any book store. If you run out of books or the store does not have your book, you will do the sales exactly the same way but, when the customer says they would like an autographed book, you explain that you have sold out and these books are for display only. However, the store will have more books in 2 days and you will autograph this book plate for them right now. Take their information on the back order form and paperclip the signed book plate to that order form (do not give the plate to the customer as they will immediately lose it). This way you can sell books even when the store doesn't have them and you will have no returns. Remember that you can only do this with Waldenbooks. Barnes & Noble and Borders must have already gotten a purchase order number from their home office or they will never pay you but their home office will be closed when you are at the store (evenings and weekends).

3. Seminars/Speaking Engagements

Everyone will tell you this is where the money is and this is the one time I agree with everybody else. Most people think it is because you get paid to do the speaking. What you get paid is a very small amount and probably will not cover your traveling expenses for any distance. For instance, of all the places I speak at around the country, I usually get an average of 30% of the attendance fees. However, this includes places where I get 50% and other places where I get zero. So why would I travel 1500 miles to teach for free? The secret to using this is that you are allowed to sell your books directly to the public (your audience) at full retail price.

This makes more money for you whether you sell your work to a publisher or if you are self-published. If you are self-published, you will be selling your books at the class at full retail price (although I do offer a small savings to encourage shoppers). If you have sold your work, there will always be a clause in your contract allowing you to buy copies of your book from your publisher, usually at a 40% discount. This means you can set up a speaking engagement, buy back some books paying only 60% of the retail price, and then sell them at your class for the full 100% making a 40% profit rather than the usual 4% royalty.

There are two important things involved in doing seminars: one is setting them up and two is what will you talk about. FICTION WRITERS – pay attention here because this applies to you just as well as the non-fiction writers.

The bad part of doing classes is that it is more difficult to get into the industry because you have to have a proven speaking record. Therefore, if you are just starting out or if you want to try out a new seminar subject, try starting with local Parks and Recreation Departments. These are plentiful as every little community has one. However, you need to call all the towns around you (or wherever you are traveling to) in order to find the ones that actually offer classes. Because these Parks and Recs do not have big budgets, you will probably start with a small class of 7 or 8 people. However, if you are not into public speaking, this is a good size group to start with to avoid feeling very intimidated.

If you would like a starter list of places to try, go to my website at www.BooksAmerica.com/seminars.html for locations and phone numbers. Keep in mind that you will probably have a lot more locations that will accept your class then mine. My husband and I specialize in our investing class on *Building Your Financial Portfolio On $25 A Month*. Keep in mind that it is very difficult for us to get engagements because most schools use local stock brokers and financial managers to teach investing classes. We have worked hard so that people know us but most schools cannot let us teach because these brokers threaten to not present any more classes if they let the Christensen's in (brokers do not want people to know about our method). Hopefully, you will not have that kind of a problem.

You will need to call to find out the name of the director for the community education department or continuing education department and their email address or fax number or mailing address (personally, I prefer using email). Then you will send them a proposal letter. On the following page is a sample proposal letter. Read this carefully as it has everything that your proposal letter will need.

It is easy to send out these proposals. It is difficult finding someone to accept your proposal. Keep in mind that you will need to follow up on these letters by phone or you

Christensen

8343 Valley Lark Drive * Sacramento, CA 95823
Phone 916-422-8435 * Fax 916-422-1918 * email ELPBooks@aol.com

January 10, 2007

Mr. Smith, Community Education
Some University

Dear Mr. Smith:

Please accept this letter and attachments as a proposal to present a class through your university.

This seminar is unique in that all other investing classes are taught by stock brokers and financial managers looking for more business. We are **not** brokers or financial managers but simply investors ourselves who have used this method for over 25 years. We have been presenting this class nationwide since 1997, the year the first edition of this best-selling book came out. Attached is our current upcoming schedule. Feel free to contact any of the directors on this schedule for a recommendation.

Building Your Financial Portfolio On $25 A Month (Or Less)

Join California best-selling authors Bobbie and Eric Christensen for an information packed seminar that will show you in easy-to-understand language how to find investments so safe that they are recession proof, yet are growing 50% to 100% in value every year, and how to do it all without using a broker. The Christensen's are not stock brokers or financial advisors but are investors just like you who have used this method for safe investing for over 25 years. In easy to understand language, they explain: WHAT your broker will never tell you, HOW to find safe and secure investments with 100% or more growth per year, HOW to invest without using a broker, WHY picking individual stocks is much safer then mutual funds, WHAT are splits, dividends, direct cash purchases, etc. and how to use them to your advantage, HOW to do easy research in just minutes, PLUS much more. *"I don't want to be taught by a broker!..the most valuable financial class I have ever taken."* (Kathryn Isacksen, St. Paul, MN) Optional book available $15.

Bobbie and *Eric Christensen*, California writers/speakers present over 100 seminars nationwide every year and have appeared on PBS' Smart Money and hundreds of other TV and radio shows. They are retired bankers and are the award-winning co-authors of the best-selling *Building Your Financial Portfolio On $25 A Month (Or Less)* and its sequel *Top 50 Best Stock Investments* as well as eight other books. You may contact the Christensen's at ELPBooks@aol.com.

Besides a listing in your catalog, we would contact our own personal mailing list (well over 500 people in your area) and do extensive media coverage. For your size area, we would expect about 25 to 35 attendees (although we have classes as large as 100). We receive a percentage of the attendance which is negotiable. However, please note on the attached schedule that each location charges whatever they want for this class.

We will be in your area this summer and would like to present this class on Saturday, June 26th, from 6:30 pm to 9:30 pm. I will call you next week about this or feel free to contact me at 916-422-8435 or email ELPBooks@aol.com

Sincerely,

Bobbie Christensen

will never hear back from anyone! Also remember that it takes awhile to build up your speaking reputation.

So, what are you going to speak on? If you have written a non-fiction book, I hope it goes without saying that you will teach your class everything you teach them in your book. However, if you write fiction, what will you speak on?

In order to write a work of fiction, you must know a lot about something or about several things otherwise you could not write that story. This is what you will teach. For instance, a friend of mine who writers mysteries does a talk on the architecture and history of Napa Valley (California's wine country) because one of her books involves finding the treasure hidden in the walls of an old hacienda. Another friend only uses knives and swords in her action/adventure books. So she gives a class filled with humor on how to kill your enemies at the semi-annual gun shows around the country. A science fiction writer who has amassed a large collection of original science fiction art from the last 100+ years does a slide presentation on the art of science fiction. Another science fiction writer speaks on "Science Fiction: Fact or Fiction" concerning what writers have predicted and what came true and what did not and why. A romance writer does "Bringing Romance Back to your 10 year old marriage" and one for men called "Anyone can wrap any woman around their little finger in 10 easy steps" and proceeds to teach them what women are looking for. Get the idea? Take what you know about in order to write your book and teach people about that subject.

Children's writers are only slightly different. You will still teach what you are trying to teach the child who reads your book, but who is your audience? Keep in mind that the majority of children's books are bought by grandparents followed by parents and then teachers (children buy very few books themselves). So you are talking to the adults. Therefore, if you are teaching children to not speak to strangers, you might give a class for the adults called "Protect your children from kidnapping". During the class you might refer to your book 2 or 3 times as in, "On page 8, my story says blah-blah-blah in order to teach children what to say if a stranger approaches them."

Always remember to give your audience every little bit of information and never hold anything back. I have found that the more I stress that a person does not need to buy my book because I am going to teach them everything they need to know, the more books they will buy.

I admit that speaking is much more difficult to break into then book signings are. However, just as with book signings, once you have done a class and have gotten good evaluations from the class, it is very easy to do the same class at the same school every 3 to 4 months. Also, your reputation will grow. People who liked your class will tell their friends about it (be sure to include attendees on your mailing list). However, schools will learn about your class from other schools. It is not unusual for me to be contacted by some college that heard about my classes from a colleague at another college and then contact me to offer a class at their school.

You will need to set up speaking engagements at least 6 to 9 months ahead of time as the schools need this much lead time for their catalogs. Any place that decides to not have you speak should be on your mailing list so they will be notified every few months of what you are doing and your ever increasing class schedule. A place I had contacted two years previously finally called me to say they had "just heard" we had an excellent seminar and would like to offer it at their school.

Some tips on speaking: be excited or your audience will not get excited, make fun of yourself and make them laugh, two or three times during your presentation refer to specific pages in your book as examples of what you are teaching, give your audience lots of information as that is what they paid for, and ***always make your audience laugh*** as laughter does sell books. And if you are really nervous about public speaking, just be yourself and pretend you are telling a me about your book. The compliments you receive at the end of your class will build your self-confidence and make you feel great and make giving the next seminar that much easier!

4. Media Coverage

Whenever you do a book signing or a speaking engagement, you need to notify the media. Actually you should be doing this all the time to get as much free advertising as you can.

There are two types of media: the print media or newspapers/magazines and the entertainment media or radio and TV. The most important in terms of number of sales is radio. The reason you need to set up book signings two months ahead of time is to give you a chance to do your mailings (see step 1 on Flyers) and to contact the media.

News Releases – This is what you send to a newspaper. As it is important to get as much media coverage as possible, you should be sending out a different news release at least once a month. However, realizing this is probably impossible with your limited time, remember that the more you send out, the more chance you have of getting coverage. You must definitely contact the media whenever you are going to do a book signing or a speaking engagement.

On the following page is a sample news release. It should be double spaced. In order to get this published, you need to give the editor's readers something very interesting or something they can learn and use in their own life. Remember that 90% of the news you hear and read came from someone's marketing department. Also, remember that a new writer with a new book is not news worthy because there are about 4,000 new books every month.

So, what are you going to write about? Think about what you are teaching people in your seminars. For instance, the romance writer might do one on the "Top 5 ways to put the

77

For release week of January 21, 2007
For review copy/media info – Susan Raymond, 916-422-8435

WHAT HAPPENS WHEN YOUR STOCK BROKER GOES BANKRUPT

Sacramento, CA – "People forget that brokers are businesses and, just like any business, they can and do go bankrupt particularly during recessions," says Bobbie Christensen, author of *Building Your Financial Portfolio On $25 A Month (or less)*. "When that happens you lose every penny of your money."

To avoid this kind of catastrophe, Christensen has been using a special method of investing for over 25 years. Brokers cannot get Federal insurance as a bank can. Therefore, they get private insurance. However, when a bankruptcy is declared, the first ones in court are the creditors that broker owes. Historically, by the time the shareholders finds out about the court proceeding, all of the insurance money is gone and the shareholder ends up with nothing.

Because of this, Christensen offers the following advice to keep your investments safe.

- Always invest in individual companies rather than mutual fund situations so you keep control of where your money is being invested. Remember, the Rockefellers do not invest in mutual funds.

- Buy your stock directly through the company in order to keep the stock in your name rather than in street name (the broker owns your stock).

- Do not take risks with your future. Only invest in safe, well established companies. No high tech.

- Any company you invest in should have safety, growth, a dividend reinvestment plan, and a direct cash purchase program.

Christensen will be presenting a 3-hour seminar based on this book at UT Austin on April 28th, at 6:00 pm, for $39. Please call 1-800-929-7889 for more information.

# # #

zip back in 10 year marriage", or a science fiction writer might do "The real Jules Verne time machine", or a mystery writer could do "Most domestic murderers use knives", or a children's writer could do the "Top 5 ways to protect your child from kidnapping". Keep in mind the usual rules of writing for your article: who, what, when, where, why, how.

The last paragraph will be advertising your class in a subtle way. Keep it short and simple: "Christensen will be presenting a class on this on May 26th. Call 1-800-929-7889 for more information." The editor can use your material and delete this final paragraph if they want to but, if you give them something good, they will usually leave it on.

You need to email these or, if that is not possible, fax them or mail them out. If mailing, be sure to hand address all envelopes so the entertainment people think it is fan mail and will at least open it up.

Radio/TV Interviews – Note the following mailer that is sent to the entertainment media. Keep in mind that these people really do not care what your book is about but only whether you can entertain their audience. Note that it is very similar to the flyer you send to your mailing list. Keep in mind that they want something controversial and remember that just about anything can be made controversial!

A host or their producer may contact you about doing an interview. Keep in mind that they are your audience and you must make them laugh (or at least chuckle) and grab their attention immediately. This is the kind of person they are looking for to be on their show, someone who will make their audience laugh and really keep their attention with interesting stories and examples. You will usually only be scheduled for 10 minutes (which is better then TV's 3 minutes anyway).

Author available for interview

See attached for upcoming personal appearances

"...always welcome here...very entertaining...phones are still ringing..." (Mike Murphy, KCMO, Kansas City, MO)

"...great personality...knows how to grab listener's attention...planned on a ten minute spot but kept her for the entire hour...funny..." (Larry Morgan, KGGO, Des Moines, IA)

"...we were getting calls for her 800 number a month after the show...very popular..." (Ron Olson, FM100, Memphis, TN)

From award-winning authors Bobbie and Eric Christensen

Building Your Financial Portfolio On $25 A Month (Or Less)
(winner of the '98 Best Business Book)

$25 per month x 10 years = $100,000

Is it possible to make thousands in the stock market with a $25 investment? Absolutely! According to author Bobbie Christensen the stock market is proven historically to be the safest way to save for the future. Christensen will demystify the market in a clear and entertaining way even a ten year old can understand. She is know to capture listeners who are cruising the dial and keep your audience smiling. They will reveal:

Why stock brokers don't want you to have this information
How investing $25 a month becomes $100,000 or more in just 10 years
What stocks are proven to keep going up no matter what the market does

"I hold nothing back. Your listeners get the whole story!"

Bobbie Christensen and her husband and co-author Eric have been using this method successfully for themselves and thousands of others for over 25 years. They are retired bankers. They are the award-winning co-authors of the best-selling *Building Your Financial Portfolio On $25 A Month (Or Less)* and its sequel *Top 50 Best Stock Investments*.

To book your show, call (916) 422-8435

However, if they like what you are doing, be prepared to be asked during the commercial break if you can stay on for another half hour or longer. I once had to stay on for 1½ hours answering call-ins because their next guest, Charlton Heston, was late (he can be late, you cannot). I sold a lot of books that day. Thank you, Mr. Heston, for being late.

As you will usually only have 10 minutes, you need to make your most important points immediately. The easiest way to keep an audience's attention is to make them laugh. You must have a toll free number that people can call to order your book (see below). HINT – The day before you are scheduled for the interview, call the station and ask the receptionist for her name and email or fax number. Then send her, in big bold easy to read lettering, "Bobbie Christensen will be interviewed by Bill Jones tomorrow at 9:30 am. For information on *Building Your Financial Portfolio On $25 A Month,* call 1-800-929-7889". People in cars have a problem writing down phone numbers and will call the station. The receptionist they will speak with is busy answering the phone and doing office work and probably did not even hear you or know you were going to be on. So give her a chance to help you.

* * * * *

To contact these newspapers and radio/TV stations, go to your public library and use the Gale Directory of Publications and Broadcast Media. These books are alphabetical by state and then by city with all print media and then entertainment media listed below. Bring your lap top with you and you can enter the information you need (state, city, name, size, email, fax, or phone number, and address) right into your computer for future use. You can buy the complete set but it currently costs about $950. I use it a lot and it is a business expense but, when starting out, I suggest you use your library.

Toll Free Number – If you are going to be sending out flyers, doing book signings, and doing interviews, you must have a toll free number for people to call to order your book. Otherwise you have just wasted your time. The cheapest way to do this is by using your printer. Most of the big Midwest printers are already set up with a toll free number you can use and they can take the orders and ship them out. Personally I do not recommend using fulfillment houses because they charge for everything including if you dare to breathe. You can also do this yourself.

You can get your own toll free number by calling you phone carrier. They can assign you a number and connect it to your home number (I suggest getting a separate business line for this). However, you will need someone to answer that phone. The least expensive way is to check your yellow pages for "answering services". You should be able to find a small one that will take orders and fax them to you at the end of the day for a set fee of about $100 a month. If you or family members are able to answer the phone all day long, this will save you quite a bit.

You will also need to be able to take at least **Mastercard and Visa.** You can get this through many places including your bank, credit union, Costco, etc. This will usually involve a one-time set up fee of $300 to $1,000 (depending on your credit history), a monthly fee of about $30, and a per charge fee of 2% to 4+% for each charge you process.

These first four steps are the most important things you can do to sell books. However, once you have those under your belt, a good business person should be thinking about how to sell even more books.

5. Diversification

How can you diversify their business in order to create more sales. The following are just a few examples:

Write another book! First of all, people love sequels. So, if you have written a non-fiction on healthy eating habits, do another one on healthy exercising. If you write fiction, take one of the sub-characters from your first book and make them the main character in a new book (people love to know what happened to these people after the book ended). If you write children's books keep in mind that readers want to see more using the same characters. However, if you do not want to write the same type of book, then just write whatever you want. It really does not matter. If people like your first book and your classes, they will want to buy your second book no matter what it is about.

Write a booklet! This is an inexpensive way to get more information out to readers. Of course, these cannot be sold through book stores or to libraries but are great for residual sales at your seminars and classes. If you offer your customer a booklet for $9.95 called "100 Ways to Enjoy Brussel Sprouts" and they like this booklet, they are more apt to order your complete cook book.

Newsletters are great if you have written a non-fiction book to keep people up to date on information on this subject. For instance, we have a monthly newsletter for our investment seminar attendees called "Common Sense Portfolio" with over 600 subscribers that pay $26 a year for it.

How about creating a fan club for your fiction writing? This involves creating a quarterly news letter letting people know what you are doing, relating funny stories, and letting them know about your new book coming out next month and your upcoming speaking engagements. If people like you and they like your books, they want to know about you.

Audio CD's are easy and cheap to produce for non-fiction books. If you check around, you should be able to find a recording company in your area that will come into one of your classes for a live recording. However, unless you are doing a children's read-along CD, the sales will be small but, as the markup is higher, it is a good residual sale. Unfortunately, doing CD's of a fiction book is very expensive.

I have a friend who writes poetry and her daughter is an artist so they started their own greeting card company. Every time they come up with a new design, they send one sample card along with an order form to everyone on their mailing list.

Consulting is a lucrative field. Personally, I have found that by offering free consulting at any time, I sell a lot more books. But for some areas, personal consulting for a fee would work best.

Write articles based on your work and seminars for publication. Even offer them for free to small newspapers and magazines so long as you get a writer's block stating, "Bobbie Christensen has 10 published books. Call 1-800-929-7889 for more information or go to www.BooksAmerica.com.

Sponsor charity events. For instance, a writer on physical fitness sponsors a walk-a-thon every year. He pays no money but uses his time to get the cooperation of the local media for free publicity (and he gets publicity also). Then he has his own table (right between the sign up tables) where he sells autographed copies of his book. It takes a lot of his time to set up but does not cost him anything as all actual costs come out of the sign-up fees.

There are lots of other things you can do but keep in mind you are only one person with only so much time to put into this. However, a few of these things will definitely help your sales.

6. Internet Sales – According to the national statistics for 2005, of all the retail sales in this country (books plus everything else), internet retail sales accounted for just 7% of the total. In other words, if you think you are going to create a web site and people will flock to your book, you better think again. The reason is that most books today are bought by people 50 years of age or older (and 90% of book buyers are women). We baby boomers are the ones who were raised reading and loving books. We all know that younger people today are too involved in computers (and TV) to read books. Thus most books are sold through the traditional ways such as speaking engagements and book signings. However, we baby boomers are getting older. As we die off and the younger people become the majority of the population, you will see the above statistics changing. I'm not worried about this because by that time I will be dead and gone. However, you younger ones need to keep this in mind that things will be changing.

Meanwhile, what is important is to have a web site simply for professional reasons. That is, if you do not have a web site, than you are not considered professional. You should be able to get a good website created for very little money (today, high school students can do this for you). What is important is to keep it simple. That is, you need a full-color copy of your cover, a good selling write up, a few reviews from readers or seminar attendees, and how to order the book. Stay away from lots of graphics as most computers out there today are at least 3 years old meaning it would take forever to download a site with lots of graphics.

However, if you are a true "web surfer", you can attract more people to your site by checking out other sites where you can put in a casual word or two about this great book you just read.

Have Fun

Keep in mind that there are three types of readers. One is the avid reader who will read just about anything in their areas of interest. The second is the person who wants the information you offer, is not an avid reader, but will buy your book in order to get the information. The third is the person who has read your first book, loved it and, whether an avid reader or not, will read whatever you produce so long as you keep up the quality of your writing.

You should enjoy what you are doing. Yes, at first, doing the marketing might be very nerve wracking because you are not used to it. However, perseverance will pay off. I can guarantee you that you will only get out of your book what you are willing to put into it. You will only make as much as you are willing to put into it. If you do all of the six marketing steps in this book, you will make a lot of sales. No, you will not become a millionaire. However, we have authors including myself who follow these steps, work hard, enjoy their work, and make $250,000 a year or more.

The purpose of this book and my nationwide seminars is to give you all the information you need about writing, publishing and marketing your book for you to make an informed decision about your book, should you write it or not. Also, I hope that you will avoid so many of the mistakes I made when I started my first book in 1995. It is now up to you. Let me hear from you. My reward is every time another person sends me a copy of their new book and thanks me for helping them. That is what makes my work worthwhile.

PART IV – Some comments on traveling in order to market your books

Although we do not have much time in classes to talk about the advantages of traveling, this seems to be of great interest for a lot of writers. That fact is, the more you can travel, the more books you can sell as you reach more and more people who will tell their friends.

However, in order to make travel pay for itself, you need to do it as economically as you do the rest of your marketing. My husband and I have been traveling nationwide (as well as overseas) for over 11 years now. Hopefully the following information will help you.

Keep in mind that, in order to make travel work for you, you need to enjoy traveling which may rule out some of you right here. However, because all travel expenses for your writing business are tax deductible business expenses, you should be aware of how to go about this. For instance, you may have to go to your niece's wedding (who you do not particularly like). You might have a miserable time there but, if you set up a book signing or speaking engagement while there, than you can make your whole trip tax deductible.

Mode of transportation – The profit from each book (if priced correctly) may be only $10 yet your travel expenses have to come out of this amount. Until you have built up your business to several books and extensive marketing, air travel will usually be too expensive for you. We fly when going outside the continental United States for seminars but do not make a profit from these trips. That is, we usually make enough from our percentage and the sale of books to pay for 80% to 90% of the trip (plus it is tax deductible). So we don't make a profit, but we do get our information out to another region and get to travel also.

We started out twelve years ago with an RV and are still RVing today. We currently have a Ford F250 truck with a Lance camper on it. This is just right for the two of us plus all the books and office things we have to carry with us for a 3 to 4 week trip cross country trip (which we do 2 to 3 times a year). If you are taking the whole family with you, we would suggest looking at a small Winnebago. Keep in mind that you do not have to buy a new unit either. If you understand motor vehicles, you can spend some time and find a good used one from $3,000 to $15,000. The equivalent new would be closer to $60,000 and up. Again, keep in mind that, if it is used for your business, you can depreciate this over several years and all the expenses involved including gas, oil and repairs, tolls, parking, etc. are tax deductible.

However, you can also usually do this with your car if it has a large enough trunk. We did use our Pontiac Grand Prix for a little over a year for this purpose but found that, due to the ever increasing cost of motel rooms, we hurried through our trips more and did not take the time to go site seeing and just spend a couple of days each week relaxing. We went back to RV'ing so we can take off a couple of days to go hiking or whatever.

Also remember that in order to successfully accomplish a weeks long trip through several states, you need to be very organized and keep your vehicle in good repair at all times.

Gasoline – As this is a very big expense in traveling, it gets a separate heading. First, get your membership in Costco and get their nationwide catalog of where they are located. This will also show whether they have a gas station or not. Most of you are aware that you will not find a better gas price then at Costco. If traveling nationwide, get a catalog of the Flying-J stations as they have lower prices, dump and fresh water stations for RVs, plus just about anything else you could possibly need.

Accommodations - If you have to stay in motels, you will have to plan on spending at least $65 a night on average (however, this seems to be going up weekly) for an economy motel. If you can plan your traveling around relatives and friends, this could save you quite a bit on the cost of accommodations.

I admit that I am personally prejudiced against motels as I just can't seem to sleep soundly unless I'm in my own bed. Our RV has the best mattress either of us has ever slept on. We feel there are many advantages to traveling by RV. For one thing, you don't have the high cost (and calories) of constantly eating out. I do not even want to discuss how much weight I put on that year we used the car! Plus, the cost of accommodations is much less.

You definitely want to get a copy of the KOA guide and the Trailer Life Campgrounds, RV Parks & Services Directory. This will list ALL campgrounds including KOA's, Good Sam Parks, private campgrounds, as well as local, state, and federal campgrounds . With a KOA or Good Sam membership, you can save 10% of each night's stay. Nationwide you will probably average about $30 to $40 a night depending on the area of the country (although these prices also creep up).

However, you will also want a Rand McNally Road Atlas as it shows where all the rest areas are. Keep in mind that in most parts of the country (the west and Midwest in particular) you can spend the night in a quiet rest area for free. We can certainly afford to pay for RV parks but like the rest areas because sometimes we are driving all day long. If staying in a motel, we have to call ahead and make a reservation to make sure we have a room for the night. With rest areas, we can drive as late as we want and then pull in for the night. Keep in mind that in the northern areas of the country and New England you will be lucky to find *any* campground open in the winter but the rest areas are open. Another free area to stay at are most Flying J's

Also, we have found that most, although not all, schools we teach at will allow us to camp overnight in the schools parking lot. This saves us driving time late at night after class and time driving back the next day for another class.

Although rest areas usually have signs saying no overnight camping, we have been told by state police that those signs give them the ability to remove people who are causing a problem. However, I would also suggest that you either travel with another person or, if you are by yourself, get a good size dog as a pet to keep you company and as a good watch dog. Unfortunately, today you need to be careful about traveling alone even when staying in motels/hotels.

Eating – If traveling by car, you will have the added expense of eating out all the time. I will admit that we still eat out when camping in Las Vegas because we love the buffets in that town. Other than that, we eat in the RV. I admit that I like cooking but, even if you do not, you can easily get a microwave for the RV and bring frozen dinners with you in your refrigerator/freezer.

We find ourselves usually stopping at a large grocery store about every 3 days to stock up on fresh fruits and vegetables. What meat we eat is usually brought from home and kept in the freezer. This means we eat much healthier by RV'ing.

One other point: it is easier to grab a snack or quick lunch when trying to make time in your driving when you can just grab something from the frig.

Things to bring with you -
Books for classes as well as to ship to wholesaler and book stores while on the road.

Envelopes for these shipments.

Flyers to handout at classes including your schedule of upcoming events and an order sheet.

Some food but you can also stop for groceries along the way.

Clothes for all climates from shorts to winter parkas, depending on where you will be going.

Office supplies such as pens/pencils, stapler, empty file folders, folders of information you may need, envelopes, stamps, a file box, etc.

Equipment such as lap top computer, portable printer, cell phone.

If traveling by car, get a good ice chest for perishables.

Bring plenty of drinking water or plan on buying bottled water.

A new Rand-McNally Road Atlas is a necessity.

Using your computer and getting email – I do not even have a desk top computer any more. I found myself having to constantly save info from the desk top computer to my lap top for a trip and then back again when we got home. I now just use the lap top for everything. However, make sure you have sufficient batteries for it and get a recharger that plugs into the cigarette lighter. Also keep in mind that you can recharge batteries in the classroom while giving a seminar.

As business people, we have to have access to our email as that is the way the majority of business is done today. Most campgrounds are providing modem connections as are motel rooms. You usually will not be able to check email every day but we have found that every 2 to 3 days seems to suffice although we do have to explain to people that we are on the road and sorry for taking so long to get back to them. Of course, we are finding more and more places where you can use WI-FI. Some state rest areas and state parks are now providing this. Obviously this service will grow and expand and become easier to use in the coming years.

If you are processing your own charges, you will need a phone line to plug the machine into. Again, you can do this at most motels and campgrounds.

Other things to plan – As to getting your regular mail, we are fortunate that our daughter lives in town and picks up our mail once a week and forwards it to us at pre-arranged schools we will be at every couple of weeks. There are services that will also do this for you or find a student that you can trust and wants to earn some easy money.

Do you have pets that need to be taken care of or can you bring them with you?

Get call-forwarding on your home and business phones so you can transfer all calls directly to your cell phone while traveling.

How will you deposit checks? Talk to your banker and get their "mail deposit" address and send deposits by Fed Ex (you will definitely need a Fed Ex account anyway for your business). Or have your business account with a nationwide bank so you will be able to find one anywhere you go.

Enjoy yourself – Finally, if you are able to travel in order to do more book signings and seminars, than you will sell a lot more books. I hope you will enjoy meeting new people and talking with them about your book as much as I do.

However, the other side of traveling is for those of you who really do love seeing new things. Plan some time for relaxing and enjoying your travels. That one year we used the car and hurried through our trips I really missed stopping at local state parks all over the country for a day or two. My happiest memories of traveling are camping at a state park right beside a lake. I spent mornings at the table writing a new book on my lap top with breaks to take a sip and look out at the beautiful view. Then in the afternoon, we would go hiking around the lake.

We also get our National Park Pass every year. We more than cover the $50 cost with the savings on all the parks we go to every year.

What more can you ask for then to be writing your books, making a good living, and traveling.